The Eden Project: A Short Story

FOREWORD BY DEREK MORPHEW
...[telling] a story that everyone can read and understand.

THE EDEN PROJECT

A SHORT STORY

BILL JACKSON

radicalmiddlepress

The Eden Project: A Short Story
by Bill Jackson

Copyright © 2012 by Bill Jackson
All Rights Reserved. Worldwide.

Published by:
radicalmiddlepress

ISBN: 9781935959243

Library of Congress Control Number: 2012932604

To Luc, Meg, and John:
Being your father has taught me that disciple-making in
the home is the greatest honor in life.

CONTENTS

Foreword by Derek Morphew i
Introduction 1
The Old Testament 9
  In the Beginning...9
  How the World Got the Way It Is 13
  Blessed to Be a Blessing 15
  The Exodus: the Salvation Paradigm 18
  The Mountain of God's Presence.....................20
  The New Eden..23
  The Davidic King...27
  The Kingdom Divides and the Prophets Speak 32
The New Testament...43
  Between the Testaments 43
  The Gospels 48
  The Birth of the Christ 48
  The Galilee Jesus...50
  The Jerusalem Jesus...57
  The Story of the Early Church 62
  The Finale 73
Now What?...77

FOREWORD

For decades, the church has tried to teach the bible through doctrines made up of a string of propositions and biblical texts taken from diverse places. Postmodern people struggle to receive truth this way. They relate better to narrative or story. The biblical writers did not think in terms of neat doctrines either. They told the great story of God, the world, and his people.

There are four trends in recent theology that reflect a new approach.

First, New Testament scholars who are engaged in the Quest for the Historical Jesus, armed with an unprecedented amount of literature from the era of Jesus (Second Temple Judaism) give primary focus to the expectations within Judaism that Jesus' message of the kingdom critiqued. In doing so they delve into the story of Israel and its growing expectations that God would soon visit his people, release them from foreign domination, and restore them to their glory and mission to the world. N. T. Wright in particular has described what he calls the controlling narrative of Israel and its fundamental worldview of creationist monotheism, covenant, Torah, Land and Temple, all moving towards this "return from exile" and the coming of the kingdom.

Second, the Biblical Theology movement has begun to publish a series of works on biblical theology (edited by D. A. Carson). The assumption of biblical theology is that the biblical narrative does have a connecting integrated unity despite its great diversity. This is closely linked to a narrative grammar or simply narrative approach to particular biblical books. In this approach, instead of giving primary attention to sources (source criticism) or editing (redaction criticism), the biblical books are viewed as finished works, what Brevard Childs calls the "final form" of the text. Biblical theology, then, gives primary attention to the intended meaning of the whole composition.

Third, different strands within the contemporary church have made it their primary goal to contextualize the gospel within the postmodern worldview. Some of these approaches succumb to the ideology of postmodernism, but others are able to critically engage with the shifts in culture without losing the integrity of the biblical message. Here, too, truth is communicated through the retelling of the story or narrative of scripture with attention to meaning and relevance in contemporary society.

Fourth, the so-called "third quest" for the historical Jesus of the last quarter century has rediscovered Jesus within his Palestinian milieu and its strong sense of the imminence of the end of the age. It is here, with Jesus' whole message and mission, that kingdom theology has begun to take central stage. Where the Protestant Reformers began with Paul's theology and then interpreted the Gospels through that lens, this theology begins with the original historical mission and message of Jesus (Matthew, Mark and Luke-Acts) and uses that kingdom lens to look at the rest of scripture. This is still a fairly recent development. Bill Jackson finds his theological peers within this exciting kingdom theology movement.

With all such renewals and discoveries of biblical content, different people play different roles. There are those at the epicenter of research and development, whose writings tend to be too detailed for the average busy Christian to fathom. Then there are those whose special gift is to take these discoveries and make them palatable and accessible to the average Christian. Here the key ability is to take a mass of detail and reduce it to a story that everyone can read and understand. This is Bill's special gift. He has given most of his public career to understanding and articulating the meta-narrative of scripture within the framework of the kingdom. Those who read his major work, *NothingsGonnaStopIt!*, or watch him teach it live or on DVD, may find the sheer depth and breadth of even that condensed story too much to take in at once.

The Eden Project has condensed the larger version still further into a truly accessible read that flows easily. For many who want to grasp this great story, this volume will be the place to start. It is truly the story humankind needs to know.

Derek Morphew, Ph.D.

February 9, 2012

Cape Town, South Africa

INTRODUCTION

I have been doing the seminar *NothinsGonnaStopIt! The Storyline of the Bible* for twenty years now. I have usually done it as a seven-hour weekend adventure but sometimes I've done it as a class. Now, since the DVDs and book have come out, I regularly get emails from people who tell me that they are showing the DVDs and want to do *NothinsGonnaStopIt!* in their small group. I have also been asked continually for something shorter. At the end of the workbook, I wrote the story in about a page and a half. I've attempted to make this booklet somewhere in-between. For reasons that will become clear as you read, I have decided to rename this version *The Eden Project* and to write it as a narrated short story.

If this is your first encounter with this material, let me share with you briefly what this is and what I am attempting to accomplish with it. In the history of the Christian church, there is a famous bishop who lived in the fourth century named Augustine. One of his young leaders came to him greatly dismayed. He was trying to disciple his young converts, but was at a loss as to how to explain the Bible to them. It was such a big book. Can anyone relate? Augustine told the young man that his readers could not understand the Bible without understanding the basic storyline that holds the Bible together. This grand play, given to us in the Bible in four great acts, chronicles God's plan for creation and his interventions into the human drama to save his people after they disobey God. And, as in all good dramas, there is a hero and a villain. In the end, God reigns as King over "history," thus making it *his* story.

Augustine went on to tell the young man that out of the rich cache of biblical stories, he needed to select only the ones that drive the narrative forward. He then would have to join these stories together into a cohesive and captivating narrative so his disciples would know the overarching plot of God's unstoppable plan. This way, as his understudies read the Bible, they could locate the text they were reading in the bigger story to see how it advances the kingdom of God. This is exactly what I have done in *The Eden Project*. I should add, however, that my goal is not only that you, the reader of this book, would know the big picture of the Bible, but that you would have a new reason to get up in the morning. Each and every one of us has a critical and unique role to play in this fifth and final act of history. As author, N.T. Wright, points out, we have no script. How, then, are we to know how our parts are supposed to go? Wright says that it is only when we immerse ourselves in the first four acts that we will be able to play our parts in alignment with the plot.

Another way to have insight into the biblical narrative is to know some of the great biblical themes that glue the story together. As you read, I want to point out six great mega-themes that you can look for as you read. Before I share what these themes are, it is important to realize that the biblical story is being told at three different levels simultaneously. The most basic level is to understand how each story speaks to its immediate historical context. The reader of the Bible needs to read every passage to try to receive the message the author was trying to convey to his original audience. Second, each biblical text needs to be understood in light of what God was doing in that moment to advance the story of his people. In the Old Testament, this story centers on the story of Israel as God's missionary people for the world (see below) and in the New Testament on the story of the true and faithful Israelite, Jesus of Nazareth, the Jewish Messiah, and his followers. Third, even as each biblical passage needs to be understood within its literary and historical context and within the larger story of the people of God, it also needs to be examined to see how it advances God's plan for Creation, which involves redemption after the advent of sin and the sending of the Messiah to fulfill God's ultimate plan in the bigger story.

Now, with that under our belt, let it be said that there are three overarching themes for what God is doing in human history. The first is the establishment of the *kingdom of God*, God's rule over his realm to fulfill his purposes for creation, which I believe to be the multiplication of his joy that God shares within the Trinitarian community of Father, Son and Holy Spirit. I use the word "establishment" because God's plan for history is opposed by an evil, spiritual being called Satan, most certainly a fallen angel and the myriads of angels (now demons) that followed him. The kingdom of God, therefore, will need to be established and made firm against all opposition by those who put their faith in the word of the eternal, creator God. The second great theme is the centrality of *Jesus*, the Son of God and prototype of the true humanity. He is also the Savior in the establishment of the kingdom of God in spite of the horrors of sin and Satan's fierce opposition. In the advent, life, death, resurrection and ascension to God's right hand as Lord, Jesus will bring to fulfillment God's purposes for the created order. Finally, the third motif in God's plan has to do with God's motive for doing all this. I have alluded to the fact that God is the hero of his own story. God, therefore, does everything for his own glory. God's glory can be referred to in different ways in the biblical narrative such as references to the honor of his name or doing things for his own sake, etc., and is the reason God is worshiped by his people. To sum up, I would say that what God is doing in human history is to *establish God's kingdom through God's Savior for God's glory*. Now, how is God going to do it?

There are also three great themes in how God will accomplish his purposes in creation. The first is that he will divide the world into different language groups in a divide-to-reach strategy in which he will break a seemingly impossible task (saving humans in unified rebellion; Gen 11.6) into smaller, doable tasks. I call this the *all peoples* motif. And what does God want with these peoples, or nations? He wants to see a reflection of his own image through their *obedience of faith*. As people from among each tribe and language trust and obey, they become living pictographs of the Trinitarian God. The astute reader might then ask how this could happen when humanity is so wicked and Satan is so powerful. The answer is that God will do it through the power of the *Holy Spirit*, the third member of the Godhead. The essence of the universe itself, therefore, is Trinitarian and will result in the delight and glory of the God, who is three in one. To sum up *how* God is accomplishing his purposes in human history, I would say that it is through *all peoples according to the obedi-ence of faith through the power of the Holy Spirit.* Let

WHAT
- God's kingdom
- God's Savior
- God's glory

HOW
- Via all peoples
- According to the obedience of faith
- Through the power of the Holy Spirit

So, if someone were to ask me what the Bible is about in one sentence, I would say that it is about *the establishment of God's kingdom through God's Savior for God's glory via all peoples according to the obedience of faith through the power of the Holy Spirit.* As you now read the story of God's glory, look for these six great themes and "glue" the pieces together for yourself.

At its heart, the bigger story of God is a story of the worldwide mission of God's people to make his name fa-mous in all the earth. It seems like a lifetime ago when I was in seminary and heard Dr. Christy Wilson, former mission-ary to Afghanistan, do a lecture on Matthew's account of the Great Commission. He pointed out that when Jesus told his apostles to "disciple all the nations." The word "nations" actually means "people groups," those who share a common ethnic, cultural, and linguistic heritage. He then quoted Je-sus' words in Matthew, "When this gospel of the kingdom is preached as a witness in every 'nation' the end will come" (24.14). Suddenly, God had my attention. The world mis-sion of the people of God was tied to the end of the world. But Dr. Wilson wasn't done yet. He then asked, "If we are to reach every people group with the gospel of the kingdom, how many groups are there and where do they live?" I sat straight up. Here was something tangible, something with Velcro on it. Who were these unreached peoples and where did they live? I wanted to know so I could go!

As if the professor knew what was in my mind, he informed us that the research at that time (1981) on people groups was that of the twenty-three thousand ethnolinguistic groups, Christian missionaries had only penetrated five thousand groups. Five thousand groups in two thousand years? The math was simple—and staggering. Almost seventeen thousand people groups had never heard of Jesus. "That couldn't be," I thought. I'd always assumed the Great Commission was almost completed.

Everyone else left the lecture hall when class was over but me. I couldn't move. I wasn't able to wrap my brain around what I had just heard. What I didn't realize was that I wasn't the only one in my generation hearing these statistics. For those that heard them, they became grit in our souls and initiated a world Christian movement that has reached more groups in twenty-five years than in all of church history combined. The website www.joshuaproject.net now lists the total groups at approximately sixteen thousand groups with almost seven thousand groups unreached, thus leaving us with the job 40 percent unfinished.

The last bastion of unreached groups lies within what is called the "10/40 window," which refers to that region in the eastern hemisphere between 10 and 40 degrees north of the equator that makes up the Middle East and Asia, the most dangerous places on earth for authentic followers of Jesus. For such a time as this, God is now speaking to *this* generation. I believe that he will raise both "goers" and "senders" in a tsunami of the Holy Spirit to carry his story to the ends of the earth—and some of us will die. But as Jim Elliot, the famous missionary martyr from my parent's era once said, "He is no fool who gives what he cannot keep to gain what he cannot lose." Jim's generation found a story worth dying for. So did mine. Now my prayer is that in hearing this story the next generation will too.

Finally, you might be asking why this was originally called *NothinsGonnaStopIt!* and why it is spelled so funny. As to how it got its name, when I first gave this material, it was done as five, half-hour lectures at our Vineyard pastors' conference in 1990. When I was doing the talk on the advance of the gospel chronicled by Luke in the book of Acts, I kept asking the audience, "Can anything stop the kingdom of God?" They were really into it and started shouting out, "Nothin's gonna stop it!" I felt after that experience that this is what I should call this presentation, if I was ever asked to do it again. I spelled it funny because this is the way we say it (for better or for worse), but it describes perfectly what all those who wrestle with God are asking: can God and his Word be trusted when the world and things in life seem so out of control? The answer is a resounding, "YES!" God is the absolutely sovereign and happy King and nothing can stop his love and wisdom from reaching all the way from the farthest outreaches of the universe to the very hairs on our heads. No one says it better than Isaiah 46.10, which is why it is my theme verse for the story of the Bible.

> I will make known the end from the beginning, from ancient times what is still to come. I say my purpose will stand and I will do all that I please.

THE OLD TESTAMENT

In the Beginning...

In the beginning, God (Hebrew *Elohim*) created out of nothing everything that existed—and he did it simply by speaking. He was showing that he was infinitely more powerful than the other so called "gods" of the Ancient Near East. To make a mockery of the battle imagery basic to pagan cosmology, the text says that the Spirit (the word "spirit" means "breath" or "wind") of God was "hovering" (bird imagery implying incubation) over the waters. God simply spoke (thus "breathed") over "the deep," the supposed realm of evil powers, and light came into being and expelled the darkness. He then proceeded to create earthly forms and fill them with life. These he called "good." The pinnacle was God's creation of humankind as male and female, Adam and Eve. The Bible says that they were created in God's very image, living images of the godhead. Now, the text says, it was "very good."

God set Adam and Eve in a garden in a land called Eden. Here they walked with God and tended the garden with him. This garden is a picture of the first temple with the garden as the inner chamber where God's presence was available to his people. Adam essentially functioned as the first king and priest ministering before God and serving him. Later, the same Hebrew word for "tend" is used of the priests ministering before God in Israel's temple.

The text makes two assumptions about Adam and Eve: (1) they had a right vertical relationship with God because they walked and worked with him every day, and (2) they had a right horizontal relationship with one another, as they were naked and not ashamed. On this foundation, God gave them three assignments: (1) to multiply his image through childbearing, (2) to fill the earth with that image, and (3) to rule the earth as God's ambassadors. To ensure their success, God "blessed them." We don't know what this blessing was, but later in the story God's blessing was regularly associated with a fresh impartation of the Holy Spirit.

The text doesn't tell us why God did all of this, creating the universe, the world, and human beings to image him. We do know that, as God's people multiplied and filled the earth with fellow image-bearers, the earth would reflect God's image and glory. Later the prophets would say that at some point in human history the knowledge of the glory, of the Lord would cover the earth as the waters cover the sea. The Bible is clear that God does everything for his glory, but is not remiss or arrogant in doing so. This is a statement that there is no other being in the universe with whom to be more delighted. It is only right, then, that God should do all he does for his own glory and revel in those human beings that recognize this and worship him. The New Testament will show that Jesus is the preexistent reflection of the Father who will correct the problem of sin, which we will soon see entering into the story and, as the prototypical human, will give the world a new start. The Spirit of God seems to personify the love that the Father and Son have for one another. From the perspective of the New Testament, we could surmise theologically that God created the world that it might reflect him and multiply the joy of Trinitarian life to all that would receive it.

As we jump back into our story, we remember that Adam and Eve, on the foundation of their two assumptions, were given a blessing to fulfill three assignments, to multiply God's image, fill the earth with it (and so multiply God's joy), and rule the earth as kings and queens enacting and overseeing the plan of God. In essence, they were to expand the borders of the Garden of Eden until it filled the whole earth. One might call this great work the *Eden Project*. At the very end of the Bible, in the book of Revelation, the New Jerusalem descends out of heaven to the earth. Besides its immensity, what is most noteworthy is that this end-of-days temple has no other chambers but the inner chamber of God's presence. The Eden Project has been completed and God's presence and image fill the whole earth as the waters cover the sea. The end of the Bible recapitulates the beginning. There is one God, one plan, and one story.

In the garden, Adam and Eve were at perfect rest because every one of their needs was met in God. The fulfillment of the Eden Project would mean that this rest would span the globe. As David would later write, "He makes me lie down in green pasture." Now here was a purpose for the ages. God was so confident that the Eden Project would be completed that he himself sat down to rest. He would not need to create another thing.

After God's rest, however, came humankind's test. Satan,

in the form of a serpent, visited Adam and Eve and tempted them to doubt the word of God and devise a plan to get their legitimate needs met in an illegitimate way, thus asserting their independence and walking out from under God's blessing to carry out the Project on their own. It didn't work and humankind—as well as the Project—fell into the deep darkness of sin. God said that because they had asserted their independence, Adam and Eve would surely die, just as a branch dies when broken from the tree.

God suddenly appears to be in a seemingly impossible dilemma. As the sovereign Creator, he had issued a command that humankind would, on the foundation of right relationships with God and others, multiply God's image, fill the earth with it, and rule the earth as God's ambassadors. But now, to be true to his word, Adam and Eve would surely die. How could God fulfill his purposes if the man and woman were dead? How could he be true to his justice and his purposes for humanity at the same time? Certainly God had painted himself into a corner. From a finite perspective, the Eden Project had failed. Perhaps God is not as smart or powerful at it had first seemed. This is what the serpent had told Eve.

The reader is shocked that the man and the woman did not die for their sin. Instead, God substituted the death of animals for them and used the skins of those substitutes to cover their nakedness. Furthermore, God told the woman that she would have a male child who, though incurring a wound in battle with the serpent, would crush its head and destroy its works. God caused the serpent to slither on its belly all its days, the ancient sign of a vanquished foe. God then said that he would put enmity, or war, between the offspring of the woman and the offspring of the serpent. The storyline of the Bible, then, traces the war between these two seeds. Despite all Satan's attempts to stop the Eden Project, God's purpose would prevail because, as Creator, God spoke everything that exists into being and, as King, rules over his realm. God's answer to his seemingly impossible dilemma is that he would issue the death penalty, thus being true to his justice. But then, unexpectedly, he would bring the dead back to life out of his ability to create out of nothing and rescue not only Adam and Eve but the Eden Project itself. Life-out-of-death—that was the key. God even built that motif into nature itself. Jesus said that it is only as a seed dies that it will bring forth fruit.

How the World Got the Way It Is

Humankind, while preserved from certain death, went on to become a strange mixture of dignity and depravity, dignity as those created in God's image with capacity for great beauty and creativity, and depravity because the default nature of men and women would now be wicked rebellion. Cain, the firstborn son of Adam and Eve, murdered his brother Abel. It had only just begun.

Genesis 6 begins with the most agonizing description of the results of sin anywhere in the Bible. Sin was so powerful that despite advances in population and culture the writer of Genesis says of the people of that era, "...*every* inclination of the thoughts of their hearts was *only* on evil *all* the time" (italics mine). The Lord was grieved that he had made man on the earth and his heart was filled with pain." The same righteous God, who had been true to his character and judged sin in the garden, stood once again against sin. Brought to the brink, God's wrath finally spilled over in the return of the earth to darkness and the waters of chaos at creation. It rained for forty days and forty nights, so long that the whole earth was covered with water once again.

To preserve the seed, however, God's grace reached out to save a man named Noah and his family. Just as the man and the woman had been kept from judgment and their nakedness covered, so now Noah was protected from certain death and shut into the ark by the Lord as it rained for forty days and forty nights. As the waters receded, God reiterated the same commands to Noah that he had given to Adam. Noah's loosing of a dove off the ark to search for dry land depicts the dawning of a new creation. The astute reader notes the connection between the dove and new creation and the hovering Spirit in the original creation. Noah and his seed then proceeded to repopulate the earth, albeit now multiplying a fractured image that defaulted to sin despite Humankind's amazing potential for creativity.

As a pledge that sin would never progress to the point where God would need to reboot the system again, as he did with the flood, the God who said, "Let there be light" put his "bow" (symbolizing war) in the sky. It was as if he was laying his weapon on his heavenly mantle saying, "Never again." We can still see the colors of his light after a rain reminding us that God will bring the Eden Project to completion. This is the first of seven covenants in the Bible. Since creation took seven days, the number seven is the number of completion, or perfection in the Bible. That there are seven covenants means that God's plan will deal with sin perfectly, thus removing the barrier that keeps humans from knowing God and fulfilling our destiny as image-bearers and kingdom ambassadors who will complete the Eden Project.

As we return to our story, we now find that Humankind has settled in one place, rather than scattering throughout the earth as God had commanded. Speaking the same language they sought to make a name for themselves, rather than for the Creator, and defiantly began to build a tower so high it seemed to reach the heavens. Strangely, they covered the tower in waterproof pitch, probably as flood insurance—they weren't buying the rainbow in the sky thing. The Eden Project had now been rejected for the Asphalt Project and the people built their urban jungle ever higher.

God knew that if they continued in their rebellion, it would be almost impossible to reach them. To prevent this, he caused them to speak different languages so they couldn't communicate. This, of course, put an instant stop to the tower. That place came to be called "babel," the Hebrew word for "confusion." The Asphalt Project would ultimately fail and is depicted in the book of Revelation in the fall of the great city of "Babylon" (Rome), the writer John's metaphor for the fall of Satan's typological system of evil and ultimately a picture of the crushing of the serpent's head.

Speaking different languages, the people were forced to migrate outward in their nations, their clans, and their languages to the lands God had established for them. The reader might be wondering how the Eden Project would ever be completed with the world now divided the way it was, each national group thinking that its cultural standards and language were at the center of God's world. Humans seemed farther from God's purpose than ever…but God had a plan that nothing could stop.

Blessed to Be a Blessing

God then appeared to a man named Abram, a seemingly random face from among the arrogant and racist peoples of the earth. God told Abram to leave his land and people and migrate to the place that God would show him. If he did this, God would bless him and give *him* a great name (remember that the Asphalt Project people were attempting to make a name for themselves). God would cause Abram to multiply into so many descendants that they would outnumber the stars of the sky. But not only this—every clan on the earth would be blessed with Abram's blessing. Not everyone would receive Abram's blessing, however. To protect his people and to judge evil, God also said that he would curse those who cursed Abram's seed.

Now, at last, the reader discovers why God broke the world up into different language groups. He took a large, seemingly impossible task and broke it into smaller tasks in a divide-to-reach strategy. Abram and his seed would become God's people for the sake of the world, the puzzle piece that would tie the Eden Project together.

After God had built Abram into a people, he would commission them to go to other peoples to extend God's image and kingdom. From there, God would raise up others to go out from that people, and so on. The Old Testament is clear that the Gentiles had always been intended to be a part of the Project team, even though their full inclusion would await a Jewish missionary by the name of Paul. To a people, through a people, from a people—that was the plan. In the Old Testament, the clans would come *to* Zion to find God while in the New, God's people would go *out from* Zion until the knowledge of the glory of the Lord covers the earth as the waters cover the sea (Hab 2.14).

At the heart of the mission was the dissemination of the divine word about how God was going to deal with the problem of sin that would remove the barrier between God and men and restore the Eden Project: *remove and restore*—that's where things were headed. The removal of sin would center on the promised male child who would pay for humankind's sin and be raised from the dead out of God's ability to create out of nothing. With sin removed, the Project would take off at warp speed and would be energized by an impartation of the Holy Spirit worthy of the end of days. With the seemingly impossible task broken down into smaller, more doable tasks, God's people would go to a people, through a people, and from a people until all the clans on earth would join in imaging God and taking dominion over the earth. As God said through Isaiah, "For my own sake, for my own sake I do this...I will not yield my glory to another" (48.11). God *would* be glorified. It was certain, breathtaking—so breathtaking it would go on to capture the minds and hearts of people of every kind. With the Project's foundation laid, let's pick up the story to trace the lives of those who understood what it meant that humans were "crowned with glory and honor" (Ps. 8.5) and gave their lives to reach out to seize the future by faith.

The cast in Genesis foreshadows the world mission of the church by portraying over fifty different nations interacting with the people entrusted with the Project. There was one problem, however: Abram and his wife, Sarai, were barren. God told Abram that if he would take the name Abraham ("father of nations") by faith, the couple would have a child. Abram believed God and God credited it to his account as righteousness. From that time on, Abram was called Abraham and Sarai was called Sarah ("princess"). They were now royalty, typological king and queen of a new nation that would be known in history Israel, and after the exile as the Jews. In their faith, Abraham and Sarah did have a child in their old age, when Abram's body was "as good as dead" (Rom 4.19). When Sarah gave birth at the age of ninety, they called the child of the promise Isaac ("laughter"). Even in her unbelief, God blessed them and reiterated that they would sire a progeny that would outnumber the stars of the sky, just as God had promised. The seed would transfer from generation to generation against all odds—from Adam to Noah to

Abram to Isaac, and then to Jacob. Jacob would then pass the blessing to his son, Judah. At the end of his life Jacob prophesied that Judah's seed would produce a king whose rule would never end. He would be a lion of a man, the Lion of the tribe of Judah.

The Exodus: the Salvation Paradigm

Driven to Egypt by a famine, God rescued the twelve sons of Jacob and their families from sure extinction through Jacob's son, Joseph, whom his brothers had sold into slavery out of jealousy. God raised him up from his lowly position to sit at the right hand of Pharaoh himself. In this way, God preserved Jacob's seed for the sake of the Project. After Joseph died, the Pharaohs to come forgot Joseph and the sons of Jacob and they became slaves for four hundred years. When it seemed that it couldn't get any worse, God's people cried to the god of their ancestors for deliverance. The Bible says God "remembered" his covenant with Abraham, Isaac, and Jacob, whose name God had changed to "Israel," meaning "struggles with God." What a perfect name for the historic people of God. We continually struggle to trust him, because sin makes us arrogant, yet fearful. From this point forward God's people would be known as Israel and the ways of God would be a constant struggle for them. Isaiah would later say:

"For my thoughts are not your thoughts,
neither are your ways my ways,"
declares the LORD. (Is 55.8).

The foundation had been laid. It was time to redeem the sons of Israel and form them into the missionary people for the world.

We see in the exodus a picture of God coming to rescue humanity from slavery, typifying our bondage of sin. How did he do it? He raised up a deliverer, a type of Christ, to issue a series of ten plagues, each one a defeat of one of the Egyptian gods. God took what each god was supposedly good at and caused their specialty to go haywire, thus showing his superiority over all the lesser gods (really demons). The only reason that Israel was not judged by God along with the Egyptians—for they were just as sinful because of our common humanity—was that those who feared God trusted in his provision of a sacrificial animal slain on their behalf. For any—Israelite and Egyptian included—that put the blood of the sacrifice on the doorposts of their house symbolizing household trust, when God's death angel visited the firstborn sons of the land that night, they would not be touched. Not even the son of Pharaoh was exempt. In this tenth and final plague, God demonstrated ultimate victory over all cosmic powers. God alone was King.

As a picture that they were not to linger in the land of sin and slavery any longer, they ate a meal that would henceforth be called "Passover" that was to be celebrated annually. It was eaten with staffs in hand, shoes on, and their cloaks girdled up so they could run…run away from sin and slavery toward the divine presence lost in the garden. When the morning came, the sound of wailing was heard for the firstborn sons of Egypt. Pharaoh finally relented and gave Moses and those who feared God permission to follow him out of Egypt. Israel went up with a "mixed multitude" because many Egyptians had also been convinced by the "signs and wonders" of Israel's god that he had no equal. To go up out of Egypt with their former slaves suddenly became the smartest thing to do. From Israel's inception as a nation, then, we see God's people fulfilling their missionary calling to be a blessing to the nations; being a part of the people of God has never been an issue of racial heritage, but of faith.

As if to make it doubly obvious that it was God who was

redeeming them from Egypt, he brought Israel to the edge of the Red Sea with no place to go. We are here taken right back to the opening verses of Genesis where the deep represented chaos, the mythic realm of evil. But once again, God sent his breath and blew back the waters so his people could walk "through the valley of the shadow of death" to a "table prepared before them in the presence of their enemies" (Ps 23.4-5). When they passed through the waters up on to dry land, Pharaoh, having now come to his senses, realized that he had just let his entire labor force go and presumptuously tried to follow them into the deep. Once again, God drew upon the ancient battle motif and released the waters simply by withholding his breath and cursed those who dared to curse Israel (Gen 12.2). The Israelites rejoiced at God's just judgment and sang from the opposite shore, "the horse and rider fell into the sea." It was then that they finally saw it. God had just defeated *every* foe. He called himself "Yahweh," the God who was "ever present for them" (the probable meaning of the Hebrew consonants YHWH). Yahweh, the God of Israel, was also Elohim, the Creator (the name for God in Gen 1.1), and King over the entire universe. In the first explicit reference to the Kingship of Yahweh, the mixed multitude declared, "Yahweh will reign forever and ever (Ex 15.18).

The Mountain of God's Presence

God then brought the people he had created and redeemed to Mt. Sinai, the mountain of his presence and a type of the Garden of Eden. This time there was no walking with Adam in the cool of the day. Because the shroud of sin choked the earth, the new Adam, the Prophet Moses, had to ascend the heights to find God amidst thunder, lightning, and thick darkness. The people stayed at a distance, weak at the knees. It was here that God gave Israel her formal missionary call. God had brought them to himself on eagle's wings to know and worship him. They alone, among all the peoples of the earth, were to be his treasured possession (Ex 19.6). They would have a regal calling—to be a kingdom of priests that would mediate between God and the other language groups to bring them the news of God's sacrifice for them in fulfillment of the promise to Abraham. Israel was to be a holy people that would model for the rest what it looked like to image God and rule as his royal representatives so the earth would reflect the glory of God.

To get them ready for their mission, God gave them a field manual called the Law that gave explicit instructions about how to approach him in the proper manner through the administration of a system of substitutionary sacrifices. The blood of bulls and goats would temporarily satisfy God's justice until the world was ready for the male child who would one day come as the final sacrifice and crush Satan's head. Later, the apostle Paul would say that when the Christ was born, it was in the "fullness of time" (Gal 4.4). The manual also taught the people of God how to treat one another with love within their cultural context. What imaging God would look like would change as cultures changed, but the principles of loving God and neighbor were the same. On that foundation, the people of God were to expand the borders of the beatific garden into the weed patches of the earth. That was their mission. It is also ours, Jews and Gentiles that trust God in Christ in the modern era, for the job has yet to be completed.

Most amazing of all was that even though God was King over the universe, he left his celestial home to live among his people and lead them forth into the Project. His desire was relational, to dwell with his people to rule over his realm. He would also transition them away from fighting with swords and teach them how to fight with light. God would lead his people from a humble, earthly palace, a mobile mission tent called the tabernacle. He presided over the universe from his throne room, the inner chamber called the Most Holy Place. The throne on which he "sat" (later they said it was his footstool) was a box made of acacia wood and covered in gold. Inside the box was the field manual and God would preside over Israel's fidelity to its prescriptions until the job was done.

Disciplinary "curses" would come to those who failed to represent God's image before the nations. Through the sting of those curses, it was hoped that those who lacked faith would come to their senses. For those who trusted God and continued to herald the fame of God's name, there would be a continual flow of individual blessings, spelled out in the so-called Wisdom literature of the Old Testament, like the book of Proverbs. Even though the nation could incur God's discipline for collective disobedience, those men and women who individually trusted and obeyed God would experience blessing in the midst of national judgment. Those who served God in leadership were given impartations of the Spirit of God to ensure their success. Once, as Moses' leaders prophesied under the power of the Spirit, Moses saw this as a picture of what God wanted for all his people. He "wished" that a day would come when all God's people would prophesy under the power of the Spirit. They would have to wait a long time for Moses' prophetic wish to come true…but it would.

One of the pressing questions for the generation that had come out of Egypt had to do with where they were going and whether there would be any rain when they got there. Egypt had a predictable rainy season with an annual overflow of the Nile River that fertilized the delta. With an abundance of food, provision was seldom in question. Would their future home have the same certainties? To assure his people, God promised to send them to a land overflowing with "milk and honey" (agricultural abundance) that would have two rainy seasons each year. The first would be in the fall and would cause the newly planted seeds of the grain harvest to germinate. The last one—a greater rain—would be in the spring and would bring the harvest to fruition. These would prove to be important promises, because other nations would attempt to persuade the Israelites that only their gods could be trusted for rain, especially during periods when God was testing his people with one of his disciplinary curses in the form of droughts. The question during times such as this was *who* would provide for Israel?

The answer was Yahweh, the God of Israel, Elohim and Creator of the entire universe. It was no contest—but would they trust him or turn to other gods?

The New Eden

Everything had now fallen in place. God had created a people for himself and had defeated the gods that had held them captive through the prophetic ministry of one from the seed of Abraham. Death had passed over God's people because they had trusted in God's gracious provision of a substitutionary sacrifice. God had then resurrected them from certain death and carried them on eagle's wings to the mountain of his presence. Throughout the biblical story we will see the recapitulation of the life-out-of-death motif that will be the way that God will resolve his seemingly impossible dilemma. As the resurrected, multi-ethnic people of God, he then commissioned them to bear his image to the nations and set up his palace from which he would rule and lead his people. But to where?

God told Abraham that he was going to carve out for

Israel a new Garden of Eden from among the weed patches of the earth, a land called Canaan, later known as Israel. In this garden, God would grow a hybrid seed that would be so hearty it would be able to take root in any of the hostile soils of the earth. The Promised Land, then, was a practice run for the ultimate completion of the Eden Project at the end of the age that we will see in the book of Revelation. God told Israel's new leader, Moses, to send twelve spies into the land, one for each of the twelve tribes of Jacob. Their job was to scope out the land's bounty from top to bottom, to fuel their vision for their future for the whole earth. Unfortunately, in unbelief, ten of the twelve focused on the clans that would oppose them. As the spies came back to a waiting Israel with huge clusters of grapes and wild honey, typologically a picture of asking that the kingdom would come on earth as it is in heaven, the ten lamented that it couldn't be done. Only two men, Joshua and Caleb, refused to let the past dictate their future and declared, "We can surely do it!"

Before taking possession of cities they had not built and eating flocks and fields they had not raised, God used his people to pronounce judgment on one of the more persistent and evil Asphalt Projects on the earth. Like those who had been building the tower, these men and women, called the Canaanites, were like a cancer on the earth and were ripe for a replay of Noah's flood. If their Project were left unattended, God knew that "almost nothing would be impossible for them" (Gen 11.6), as with those building the tower at Babel. Out of his heart for the world, God issued a command for his people to execute a full seizure of their land, their lives, and their culture, thus putting a stop to the endless slabs of asphalt that would eventually cover the earth as the waters cover the sea.

Just prior to taking the first city in the new Eden, the Israeli general, Joshua (*Yeshua* in Hebrew, meaning "salvation"), had an encounter with "a man" with a drawn sword. Joshua, no doubt with his hand on his scabbard and his knees squared for battle, wanted to know if the soldier was for Israel or for the Canaanites. The man then identified himself. Here, before Joshua, stood the commander of the armies of the Lord. While the text does not identify who the commander is, we most certainly have here a pre-incarnate appearance of Jesus. *Jesus* is the Greek translation of *Yeshua*. It appears that the Pre-incarnate One wanted to remind his forerunner that Israel had been chosen *for the sake of the world*. In response to Joshua's question, the man replied, "Neither." All that God had been doing with Israel had always been for the world; the blessing given to Abram had been for all the clans of the earth. As God would later say through Amos to prevent the people of Israel from having higher estimations of themselves than they ought:

> Are you Israelites not the same to me as the Cushites?" says the Lord. Did I not bring Israel up from Egypt, the Philistines up from Caphtor, and the Arameans from Kir (Amos 7.9)?

Israel was not God's treasured possession because she was loved more. She was God's treasured possession because one nation had to be first; Israel's honor is the privilege of place in the Project, not her intrinsic purity. She was never to lose this perspective lest she herself be caught in the clutches of racism and find her fig tree barren of a harvest among the nations at the time of the male child's visitation.

In issuing his just judgment against the Canaanite's Asphalt Project, God's heart was just as filled with pain as at the time of Noah. To bring the point home, God had Israel renew her commitment to the instructions in the field manual before taking Jericho. God went first into another mock battle, as at creation, and led his people from his throne in his mobile war tent. Israel followed in worship and the walls of the first Asphalt city came crashing down. The next stage of the Eden Project had begun.

In telling the Old Testament story, a major mistake is often made at this point. It is assumed that at the time of the conquest, the new Eden had been secured when the book of Joshua comes to a close. Nothing could be further from the truth, because God's just judgment on the Asphalt people had only just begun. In reality, Israel had only entered Canaan and divvied up the land allotments for the twelve tribes. Throughout the period of the Judges, Israel lived side-by-side with these people and did not press in to finish the conquest. The Eden Project, therefore, was on hold. The story awaited a true leader who would trust God fully and finish God's just judgment against the Canaanites by securing the borders of the land. Only then could God's plan for the world move forward. Despite God's provision of "judges" that were filled with the Holy Spirit, because of Israel's unbelief, God's people were locked in a sin-repentance-deliverance-sin cycle. It seemed as if God's true leader would never arise. The book of Judges closes with the writer concluding that "everyone did what was right in their own eyes." The sons of Adam and Eve were still asserting their independence from lack of trust in the word of God. Every man was for looking out for himself—the foundational mentality of the Asphalt Project built on the foundation of Adam and Eve's decisions to walk independently from God.

As we come into the time of the last judge, a prophet named Samuel, it is clear that God is perfectly capable of leading his people as King. He alone defeated the Philistines as their god, Dagon, shattered before the throne of God's presence that had been captured and brought into their Asphalt Project temple.

It was also clear that God could use his people as he executed his just judgments. God's defeat of the Philistines in the next round of the occupation came about as Samuel obeyed God's instructions perfectly, just as Joshua had done at Jericho. Again the reader is shocked to learn that the people of Israel asked Samuel to anoint a human king "to be like the other nations." To be like the other nations? Israel had completely forgotten what they had been called to be. They were the people of God, chosen for the sake of the world. Finishing the conquest by securing the borders of the land was the necessary next step for God to cultivate the new Eden with its hybrid seeds that would take root and grow among the hostile soils of the earth. Jesus would later say that this seed would indeed grow among the weeds and at the end of the age, he would separate the wheat from the chaff. The wheat would be gathered to eternal life and the chaff would be burned and destroyed forever.

God conceded and gave Israel the kind of king they were looking for. God instructed Samuel to anoint a tall, impressive man by the name of Saul as Israel's first, human king. While Saul was striking on the outside, he was insecure and narcissistic on the inside, even to the point of building a monument in *his* image. His was the DNA of the Asphalt Project and he fell quickly. Would God appoint another king? If so, would he be one that God could use to advance the kingdom of God? In order to do so he would have to understand who God is and what he had called Israel to be. God then instructed Samuel to anoint a shepherd boy named David from the tribe of Judah to be the next king of Israel. He loved God and was as skilled with the harp as he would have been with his shepherd's crook.

The Davidic King

After his anointing by the Spirit, David was introduced to Israel as he brought supplies to his brothers who were fighting in Saul's army. The Israelites were defending the valley of Elah, a key valley for the protection of the strategic high country. Above lay a Canaanite city known as Jebus. For forty days, the biblical number of testing, the Philistine champion, a giant named Goliath, taunted the armies of Israel. As David assessed the scene, he realized that Goliath stood as a type of those among the Asphalt Project that would curse Israel, just as God had predicted in his initial encounter with Abram. Dressed in his scaled armor, Goliath also had the appearance of that serpent of old, Satan, who had also defied the very person of God. Taking it all in, David must have had a moment of revelation—God *would* curse those who defied the armies of the living God!

Drawing upon the weapon of a shepherd, David killed Goliath with one smooth stone from his sling, and just as Pharoah's horse and rider fell into the sea, Goliath fell before David. David then cut off Goliath's head with the giant's own sword as a prophetic picture of the male child who would one day crush the serpent's head. David then did an interesting thing with Goliath's head. The text says that he took it to a spot outside the gates of the city Jebus crested on the hills above. What did he do with it? The text doesn't tell us. What we do know is that later, when David reigned as king, he issued God's just judgment on the Canaanites in Jebus and chose their city as his capital. He renamed it *Jerusalem*, the city of Peace. Later, called *Zion*, it became not only David's capital, but also the city of God's presence in the land of the new Eden. A thousand years later, Jesus died outside the city gates in a place called Golgotha, the skull.

It was David, then, a man after God's own heart, who obeyed God by faith and finished the occupation that had begun during the time of Joshua. In great celebration, David brought the Ark of God into Jerusalem where he put on priestly garments and danced before the Lord. In doing so, he was a king functioning also as a priest; a king/priest prophetically picturing God's entrance into Jerusalem, the city out of which God's Israel mission to the would commence. David, then, was a kind of new Adam, the prototypical human and Israeli priest standing against sin in the zeal of Phinehas. Perhaps now the Eden Project could move forward.

In the fashion of ancient Near Eastern kings that built their gods temples after subjugating vassals in battle, David wanted to do the same for the God of Israel after finally securing all of Israel. Through the prophet Nathan, however, God told David that it was not he who would build a house for God, but God who would build a house for him. God would establish David's family line *forever*. It was not David, therefore, who would build the new temple, but a son of David. David's job had been to obey by faith and finish God's judgment against the people of the Canaanite Asphalt Project by securing the borders of the New Eden. The son of David who would build the temple would be a man of a different calling. He would be a man of peace, not a man of war. As a sign of his amazing grace, God selected Solomon to be the next king, the son of David's tragic relationship with his wife Bathsheba (David had killed her husband to have her). The name "Solomon" is derived from the Hebrew word *shalom*. Shalom points to the full experience of the Eden Project, the kingdom of God.

The traveling war tent would now give way to an edifice that was not more worthy, but more appropriate to Israel's new circumstances. It was time for God to teach his people how to tend the new Garden in preparation for the day when they would go throughout the earth preparing the soil and planting the hybrid seed. God would now preside over the Project from the temple that Solomon would build on Mt.

Zion. As always, he would judge Israel according to her fidelity to the field manual and their progress toward the goal of making God's name famous among the nations of the earth.

In the first ten chapters of the book of 1 Kings, we see that all that God had planned seemed to come to fulfillment. Solomon, the son of David, *was* established as king and *did* build the temple. The structure was so magnificent that it was considered, along with Solomon's gardens (note the garden motif), as one of the seven wonders of the ancient world. Functioning as a picture of the abundance of Solomon's kingdom, 1 Kings 4 describes what life in the new Eden was like. The text says of God's people that, "they ate, they drank, and they were happy." Furthermore, it says that, "each man had his own vine and fig tree." As a nation, Israel also had peace on every side.

But it wasn't just the nation that was blessed. Solomon himself had an immense deposit of the kingdom upon him. He was a prolific songwriter and a skilled scientist, researching everything from biology to zoology to botany. His daily table was so immense that it is almost cartoonish to read about. Each day thousands of loaves of bread and meal were eaten and hundreds of animals consumed in what was certainly the most choreographed kitchen in the history of the world. All of it was a picture of life in the Eden Project. From this point on, the banquet motif would stand for the in-break of the kingdom of God and prefigure the great kingdom banquet at the end of the age when the Eden Project would be completed and God's presence would become all in all. The Passover meal foreshadowed this great meal and Jesus would use it as the Last Supper, redefining its symbols in light of his own body and blood that would be shed for all.

With the Project running on all cylinders, the reader is not surprised when the Queen of Sheba in North Africa visited

Israel because she had heard of God's fame. The writer tells us that she was so overwhelmed with the God of Israel that she put her trust in him. One might now expect that the nations would begin streaming to Zion...but that didn't happen. The Asphalt Project had crept in and threatened to destroy the new Eden.

Deuteronomy 17 records that Moses had prophesied that one day a generation would come in Israel that would want a human king. When they did, Moses listed the kinds of characteristics that such a king should have. In the list, Moses mentioned that the king should not build a big military, lest the nations get the wrong idea about Israel. Nor should he have a large harem, lest his wives cause his heart to stray from God. Neither was he to accumulate large amounts of silver and gold with all the traps along that path. Interwoven into the description of Solomon's immeasurable kingdom in 1 Kings 4 is unfortunately the mention of exactly these kinds of things. The text says that Solomon had many chariots. Modern archaeologies' uncovering of Solomon's stables attests to how many horses he had to drive them. Israel was primarily hill country. Chariots, on the other hand, were the tanks of ancient warfare and were fit for offensive strikes on flat ground. Solomon should have been witnessing to the nations, but instead he embittered them by subjugating the surrounding countries for taxation to build up his wealth. And, just as Moses had predicted, Solomon's three hundred wives and seven hundred concubines swept his heart away from God. The man of peace ruling over the city of peace threw his peace away.

The practice run for the Eden Project was beginning to whither. Apparently the temporary removal of the sin barrier through the system of sacrifices had not really solved the root issue. Human beings were sinful creatures and always defaulted to the arrogant independence of the Asphalt Project. Only when God's sevenfold covenant had played itself out would sin be removed once and for all. Only then would the plan that nothing could stop get back on track.

The Kingdom Divides and the Prophets Speak

God didn't judge Solomon's kingdom out of his love for David, but Solomon's son, Rehoboam, was a court brat who rejected the wise counsel of his father's advisors and followed the advice of his young courtiers. He subjugated the ten northern tribes and within a matter of years fomented rebellion and civil war. Just years after David had secured the borders and finished the occupation, the kingdom was divided and the Eden Project seemingly derailed.

It was at this time that God raised up men called "prophets" to call Israel back to fidelity to the field manual. God was committed to having his name properly imaged to the nations. The ten tribes that had annexed the north, known as Israel during this time, would have twenty kings before it was all said and done, but not one of them would listen to the Prophets. As God had done at the time of Noah, at the time of the tower, at the time of Egypt, and at the time of the occupation, he stood up to defend the honor of his name. God raised up the world power at the time, the mighty Assyria and her fierce king, Tiglath-Pileser III, to execute judgment on the northern tribes, because they had demonstrated such hardness of heart. While some from each of the ten northern tribes escaped to the south, thus preserving the twelve tribes as a prophetic picture of the restoration of Israel, most were dispersed as booty among the peoples in the Mediterranean basin. Here would begin the great *Diaspora*, the scattering. It would eventually produce Jewish ghettos in every city in the empire. In God's sovereign plan, as he had done with the dispersion of the peoples at the tower, he once again forced his people to fan out in all directions. In the bigger plan of God, these Jewish ghettos and their synagogues would await a man in the New Testament by the name of Paul, God's apostle to the Gentiles…but that's getting ahead of our story. Those left in the land by Assyria would intermarry with foreigners, develop their own religion, part Jewish and part pagan, and become a half-breed people living in Samaria. We will know them in the New Testament as "the Samaritans."

The two tribes to the south, known as Judah, proved to be more faithful than their brothers and sisters to the north. While they too had twenty kings, eight listened to the Prophets and the country experienced revivals during their tenures. But even these weren't enough. The power of sin once again sucked them into the vortex of the Asphalt Project and brought judgment down on their heads. The rising world power now was Babylon, led by her great king, Nebuchadnezzar. As was true at the time of the building of the tower of "Babel," the nation of "Babylon" would go on to typify Satan's system of evil in the biblical narrative. The Babylonians were smarter than the Assyrians, however, and rather than dispersing their captives for cash, they took the best and the brightest back to Babylon to enrich their own culture and workforce. Israel found herself in captivity for seventy years and longed for the day of release back to the land. Even bigger was the question as to whether the Project was even still on. If it was, had she lost the privilege of being the people of God for the sake of the world? The Prophets said it was all still a "go" and predicted that there would be a new exodus. Israel would be restored to the land and fulfill her mission to reach the nations.

As was noted above, it was during the time of the Divided Kingdom that God raised up the Prophets. These were men who were filled with God's Spirit to call Israel back to obedience to the field manual and its prescriptions for how to worship God and image him in the world. Many of their prophetic oracles spoke directly to the restoration of Israel and the reinstitution of her missionary role. We will now back up to highlight some of their greatest prophesies as the story of the Old Testament comes to a close.

In the ninth century, the issue of rain came back on the table. At the word of the Lord, the prophet Elijah shut up the heavens and they were dry as dust for three years. Instead of repenting and turning back to the Lord, the people turned to the gods of the Syrians, *Baal* and his female partner, *Asherah*. It was thought that when they had sex, their seed would fertilize the earth and bring the harvest. To hedge their bets on the fertility of this insidious pair, Israel adopted the practice of temple prostitution to "turn on" the gods so they would send the "seed." It was the ancient version of a pornographic movie. This was so dishonoring to God that Elijah called a showdown on Mt. Carmel ("God's vineyard," a metaphor for the people of God) to show his vineyard who the real God was, just as had happened back in Egypt. Lightening swallowed up Elijah's sacrifice and the heavens were shaken in such a manifestation of God's power and affirmation of the prophetic word that it is intended to remind the reader of God's revelation of himself at Mt. Sinai. It was clear that Yahweh, the God of Israel, was Elohim, the Creator of the Universe. He alone was God.

The first writing prophet appears to be Jonah in the eighth century. The book is a living parable acting out Israel's racial prejudice and rejection of her role as missionaries. Jonah refused to preach a message of repentance to the Assyrian capital, Nineveh. God was giving Assyria the opportunity to turn from her wickedness some years *before* she rose to military prominence and destroyed Israel. Like a pawn on a chessboard, God used this nation to bring judgment on Israel, a deed he would later judge them for. What should have been seen as an opportunity to enact the promise to Abram to be a blessing to the nations became a moment of shame and horror, not only for Jonah (anyone want to be swallowed by a great fish?), but also for Israel. After being spit up on the seashore, Jonah, now in the frame of mind to obey God, preached repentance to the Assyrian capital. Nineveh did, in fact, repent and averted disaster for the time being.

It was Amos who realized that Israel had become so complacent that her empty, religious rituals meant nothing to God. It was so bad that Israel's privilege of being the people of God for the world was in serious jeopardy. Amos saw that a day of darkness was coming...but it would not be for the nations. If Israel did not change *her* ways she would be judged along with those who cursed the true seed of Abram. Joined by Micah and Hosea, these northern prophets saw their predictions of annihilation come at the hands of the now ripe-for-evil Assyrians in 722 BC. The Asphalt jungle seemed to be spreading everywhere.

The ninth century prophetic giant, Isaiah, focused his work on the two salvageable tribes to the south, the most notable being Judah out of whom Jacob had said would come the Lion King who would reign forever. Through Isaiah, God said to the Judean king, Ahaz, "I will give you a sign." This sign was intended to show the king that his fear of those from the Asphalt Project would come to naught. God would cause a virgin to be with child and she would call his name "Immanuel," meaning "God with us." The child would be a shoot from the stump of Jesse, David's father (David's seemingly dead family tree), and would be a living temple, the typological fulfillment of God's traveling war tent. He would have a seven-fold (i.e., full) endowment of the Spirit of the Lord and lead his people forth to crush the head of the serpent and his works. Furthermore, in the future God would honor the backwater area called "Galilee of the Gentiles." At the time of the male child, Galilee would be a mixed area comprised of both Jews and Gentiles and would prefigure Israel's missionary role among the nations. Through this future son of David, God said that the nations living in darkness would see a great light.

In Isaiah's collection of prophetic oracles, chapters 40-66 are written as though Israel had already gone into captivity and foretell her return to the land of Israel. In these prophesies, Isaiah offers Israel "comfort" by drawing parallels to their being in exile and their time of slavery in Egypt. Just as they were captive slaves in Egypt, they were now captive slaves in Babylon. And just as God had delivered them from Egypt, Isaiah prophesied that a "way," a new exodus would be coming when once again God would lead them out of the wilderness. As he did in the first exodus, God would send a messenger/angel who would cry out in the wilderness to prepare the way for the Lord. Arrogant people would be humbled and broken people would be raised up so the Lord's way would be made straight. The word "way" will go on to have a very important significance in the story. Jesus would go on to say that he was the "way." Furthermore, the early church would be called the "Way" in the early stages of their movement out into the world.

This way, or "day" of deliverance, would be a day of "glad tidings." The word for "glad tidings" in the Greek Old Testament is *euanggelion*, meaning "good news." It is this word, usually rendered as "gospel," that the New Testament writers will use to announce the coming of Jesus and God's kingdom. Fortuitously, it would be a word that communicated to the Greeks and Romans as well, but that is again getting us ahead of our story.

And how would this new exodus come to pass? God was going to raise up a "servant." Without a full reading of Isaiah's oracles about this servant, one might think that the servant was either Israel (41-42), Cyrus, the king of Persia, a Gentile whom God called his "anointed one" (43-48), or the remnant of Israel (49-51). Indeed, all these were servants of the Lord for a time, but the true Servant is identified in chapters 52-53. At some point, God would raise up a Servant *par excellence* who would be the Savior for the sins of the whole world. In him, the sevenfold covenant would converge to defeat human sin once for all. And how would it happen? God was going to put his Spirit on this Servant, thus empowering him differently than the servants of old. This Servant would be highly exalted, yet amazingly would suffer as one who was numbered with transgressors—a very odd picture indeed. He would be pierced for our transgressions and carry our infirmities, and by his wounds "we" would be healed. Though he would be assigned a grave among the wicked he would see the light of life and be satisfied. In him life would spring out of death solving God's impossible dilemma.

Somehow, in this manner, the suffering Servant would announce good news (*euanggelion*) to the poor, give liberty to the captives, sight to the blind, and proclaim the year of the Lord's favor for humanity. All of these are signs of the ancient Jubilee, a time when debts were forgiven, and ultimately the dawning of a new creation. As we will read in the New Testament, no one except Jesus would know how it all fit together. Nevertheless, when those in exile reread these now oh-so-relevant oracles, they would have taken great comfort in them and long for their fulfillment. In the distant future, the true Servant and Messiah would echo

Isaiah saying, "Blessed are those that mourn, for they shall be comforted" (Mt 5.4).

It was Jeremiah who finally saw it—and he saw it out of his pain. God confirmed Isaiah's word to him—out of David he would raise up a righteous Branch. But wait…there was more. And here he was not building on his prophetic tradition, not even expanding it, but bursting it wide open. God showed him that the time was coming when he would make a new covenant with his people (31.31). Using the exodus as his backdrop, just as Isaiah had done, Jeremiah predicted a new exodus from exile. In this new exile, Jeremiah said that the new covenant would not be like the covenant God had made with their Jewish forefathers. This time the field manual, the Law, would not be written on tablets of stone but on the tablets of Israel's heart. There would be a New Jerusalem, the fulfillment of the Project that would reflect God's image. God would "refresh the weary and satisfy the faint" (31.25). Furthermore, all would know him from the greatest to the least and *their sins would be remembered no more*. Only in this new covenant—the seventh—would the problem of sin finally be removed. Jeremiah was so sure of this that on the eve of the Babylonian captivity, he bought a field and staked his claim in the new Israel.

Joel realized that the return from exile would not come without the outpouring of the Spirit seen by Isaiah. After a devastating locust plague, one of God's disciplinary curses, designed to bring Israel back to the image-bearing instructions in the field manual, Joel predicted that the outpouring would come not only on the Servant, but also on *all* God's people. Moses' prayer wish would come true after all. All God's people would prophesy, not just the prophets, thus indicating that the barrier of sin had been removed and that God's people had been welcomed back into the presence of

God. Through the power of the outpoured Spirit, two-way communication with God would be restored and it would be as Adam had experienced it in Eden when he walked and talked with God in the cool of the day.

Meanwhile, back in exile in Babylon, two prophetic figures loomed large in seeing a glorious future for God's downtrodden but missional people, Ezekiel and Daniel. While Ezekiel had seen in a vision that the glory of the Lord would tragically depart from God's temple in Jerusalem just prior to its destruction by Babylon, it must have been encouraging when God told the prophet that he (God) would be with his people no matter where they found themselves among the nations. God had not scattered his people randomly. He had strategically placed them among the nations because the original mandate to Adam had been to multiply God's image until the earth was filled with God and the beauty and justice that would come in a world ruled by royal ambassadors. No, the glory would surely return, and so would God's people. In a vision of a valley full of dry bones, God showed Ezekiel that Israel would rise from the dead as a nation. In another, where Ezekiel saw two sticks being joined into one, God showed the prophet that the ten tribes from the north and the two tribes from the south would be brought back together as one. He would remove their heart of stone and give them a heart of flesh. He would put his Spirit in them and they would be cleansed of their iniquity so they could image God properly to the nations among which they were scattered.

Daniel saw that one like a son of man would go into God's presence, just as the high priest did on the Day of Atonement, and receive an eternal kingdom that he would bring to the earth. This kingdom would shatter all the kingdoms of this world and would become a mountain, the historic dwelling place of God that would fill the whole earth. Moreover, the angel Gabriel showed Daniel that after a period of "sixty-nine weeks," referring to the time between Daniel and Jesus, God would (1) finish transgression, (2) put an end to sin, (3) atone for wickedness, (4) bring in everlasting righteousness, (5) fulfill ("seal up") prophecy and (6) anoint the most holy one. As the reader might expect, the fulfillment of these things would be greatly opposed. The Anointed One (Messiah) would be cut off and would have nothing. The period between the sixty-ninth and seventieth week would be characterized by war and desolation. At the end of this time an evil "prince" would come, one Daniel had seen in an earlier vision as an arrogant "little horn" (power) that would oppress the saints and commit an abomination against the worship of God. Indeed, the saints would even be handed over to him for a short period of time. This would be a time of distress such as has not happened from the beginning of nations until then. But the saints would prevail because God would graciously rule in their favor and give them the kingdom of God. In a final revelation, the angel of the people of God, Michael, showed Daniel that even though the Anointed One would die, as all humans do, there would be a resurrection of the dead at the end of the age. In the Bible's first, clear reference to resurrection life after death, Daniel saw that on an appointed Day, all the dead would rise, people from every nation. Those who had blessed the missionaries from the faith seed of Abraham would be welcomed into eternal life, but those who cursed the missionaries blessed with Abraham's blessing would be thrust away into utter darkness.

In fulfillment of Isaiah's prophesies, one of David's descendants named Zerubbabel *did* lead God's people back from Babylon to the land of Israel, albeit still under Persian rule. With the encouragement of the prophets, Haggai and

Zechariah, a smaller, scaled down version of the temple was rebuilt and the sacrificial system reinstated. Nehemiah rebuilt the walls of Jerusalem to keep the people safe and they rededicated themselves to the instructions in the field manual and their calling to image God to the nations. Despite the fact that Haggai prophesied that the glory of the latter house would be greater than the former house, the writers never record the return of the glory of the Lord to the new temple.

The prophet Malachi, standing with Isaiah, said that all these things would come to pass with the return of "his messenger" who would prepare the way of the Lord. Malachi identifies this messenger as Elijah, the prophet that had stood for the word of God against Baal four hundred years earlier. Since Elijah had not died, but had been taken up to heaven in a fiery chariot, Malachi was saying that he would return to finish his ministry and inaugurate the next event on God's eschatological timetable—"the great and terrible day of the Lord." On this day God would, at last, return to his temple. For the people of the Asphalt Project who sought to make a name for themselves, this day would be like a fiery furnace, but for those who revered *God's* name, the "sun of righteousness would arise with healing in its wings."

The Old Testament closes as a story awaiting an ending. When would the male child come who would crush the head of the serpent and lead God's people to the fulfillment of the Project? When would the son of David arise and build the true temple? When would Daniel's son of man usher in God's eternal kingdom? When would Joel's great outpouring of the Spirit occur and the year of the Lord's favor come to the peoples of the earth through the seed of Abraham? So many questions awaiting an answer...

THE NEW TESTAMENT

Between the Testaments

As we finished the Old Testament, we left a story awaiting an ending. According to Malachi, the next chapter on the eschatological time calendar would be initiated by the return of Elijah. He would prepare the way of the Lord and usher in the great and terrible day of Yahweh. He would judge those who sought to make a name for themselves, but bring healing to those who longed to make God's name famous in the earth (Is 26.8). Four hundred years later Jesus would identify John the Baptist as the Elijah of Malachi's prophecy. He would be God's sovereign choice to usher in the next phase of the Eden Project.

As we open up to the pages of the New Testament, however, we notice immediately that the landscape has drastically changed. No longer is Israel ruled by Persia but by a new world power, Rome. Jewish political parties like the Pharisees debate over the minutia of field manual interpretations. Other parties, like the Sadducees and the Zealots, have more divergent agendas. Aramaic is now the language of Israel while the language of the marketplace is Greek. And then there is the matter of that *huge* temple on Mt. Zion that began being built before Jesus was born and was still being constructed when he died. Where did it all come from? The events and changes in the ancient Mediterranean world that occurred during this time period are absent in the Protestant canon of the Bible but appear in the Catholic Apocrypha. The astute reader will want to find a copy of the Apocrypha to get a feel for the developments that occurred during this era. For brevities' sake, I offer here simply a sketch.

In 333 BC, a young Greek named Alexander the Great conquered the Mediterranean world in a ten-year period. Even though he died prematurely, Greek culture and language changed the world, so much that even the Jews began to adopt Greek ways (some more than others, as we shall see). Alexander unified the region under the Greek language, which became the "lingua franca" of the business community. No one could buy or sell without knowing Greek—and for the first time since the tower of Babel, people of different nations could communicate.

All of this produced fierce debates among the older generation about how to fight against these dangerous and ungodly trends. Their various opinions would give rise in the New Testament to the Pharisees, Sadducees, Zealots, and a separatist movement later known as the Essenes.

After Alexander died, Israel came under the control of Syria for a short while. A despotic Syrian king known as Antiochus IV thought he was a god and called himself "Epiphanes" (God made manifest). He hated the Jews and vowed to destroy their culture, even to the point of desecrating their temple by sacrificing a pig in God's throne room and sprinkling its blood on God's throne, the Ark of the Covenant. He made Jerusalem a police state and rededicated the temple to Zeus. A young Jew named Judas, later nicknamed *Maccabee* in Aramaic, the hammer, came to the rescue and led a rebellion against Syria, recaptured Jerusalem, and rededicated the temple to Yahweh three years to the day after it had been desecrated. This began a period of Jewish independence led by the descendants of Judas. It would not last long.

Antiochus Epiphanes stands in the long line of those from the seed of the serpent—those that arose to become the Asphalt People—that have sought to annihilate God's missionary people and stop the Eden Project. He is a type of the Pharaoh, Goliath, Tiglath-Pileser III, Nebuchadnezzar, and many more down through human history. There is, indeed, "enmity" between the seed of the woman and the seed of the serpent, but as God said through Isaiah, "My purpose will stand and I will do all that I please" (Is 46.10). Nothing was going to stop the plan of God. As a matter of fact, when the Roman king of the Asphalt People, Caesar Augustus, subjugated Israel in 63 BC, God used the changes he initiated to make the final adjustments necessary for the birth of the Christ (*Christ* is Messiah, "the anointed one," in Greek).

Under the leadership of Augustus the Roman Empire expanded as far as Gaul to the west, Germany to the north, Arabia to the east and Ethiopia to the south. His great accomplishment was that he brought peace to the region for the first time in history, and because of this he was called the "savior of the world." He went on to establish the *Pax Romana*, the peace of Rome and built a new road system that connected the major centers of the Empire. By dispatching

Roman soldiers at strategic points along the roads he ensured safe travel for Roman citizens.

Initially, Rome ruled Israel through local rulers called "kings." The king of the Jews at the birth of Jesus was from Idumea, a land north of Israel. He is known in history as Herod the Great. It was Herod that built the magnificent temple that we find in the gospel stories. It was also Herod who killed all the babies in and around Bethlehem when he learned from Magi (astrologers) from the East that this was where it had been prophesied that the Christ (Greek for Messiah) would be born. The Magi represented those from among the Gentiles (non-Jews) that would "bless" Abraham (the Jews) and join the Eden Project through their witness as God's missionary people. These Magi were among the first fruits of what would become a worldwide harvest among thousands of Gentile peoples.

In Galatians 4.4 Paul writes, "When the time had fully come, God sent his son…." The Greek word for "time" used here does not mean, "ticks on the clock," but when all the factors came into alignment for something significant to occur. It is now time to see how God had prepared the world for the birth of the Christ. We saw at the beginning of the story that the power of sin was so great that God rebooted creation by bringing it back to its watery and chaotic beginnings. By his mercy he "graced" Noah to live a godly life and preserved his seed. In doing so, he initiated a plan to deal with sin through seven covenants so the Eden Project could come to fulfillment. The knowledge of the glory of the Lord would, indeed, one day cover the earth as the waters cover the sea (Hab 2.4).

As sin ran rampant at Babel, God confused human language and scattered the Asphalt People around the globe, thus creating a worldwide mosaic of rebellious and racist people groups. God then chose one man, Abram, from among these rebellious peoples and blessed him—but with blessing comes responsibility. Abram was blessed to be a blessing to all the peoples of the earth. God warned him, however, that while some would welcome the good news heralded by the Jews, some would reject the blessing and curse it. The seed of the woman would continue to be at enmity with the seed of the serpent, all the way to the end of the age. God's people should expect a great and violent pushback.

God then gave this people, the Jews, a revelation of his great name and a field manual to show them how to image him on the earth in any cultural context. But, as the power of sin also threatened to derail God's people, God scattered them, too. He sent them everywhere, not only to humble them, but to position them. Through the scattering he created Jewish ghettos in urban centers throughout the earth, each with a synagogue, each with a field manual, each praying prayers of repentance as had been prayed by Nehemiah (1.6), and each waiting for God to fill the temple in Jerusalem with his presence once again. The Jews between the testaments thought that God would come to restore Israel to her former glory and the nations would flock to Jerusalem to become Jews and find God. This was their perception of how the Eden Project would be fulfilled, but God had other plans. He used four Gentile nations to change the world and prepare it for God's time of visitation. God had shown the prophet Daniel that the Jew's Babylonian conquerors would give way to Persia, Persia would give way to Greece, and Greece would give way to Rome.

When Alexander the Great conquered the world, he unified it under one language. Those who knew Greek could not only buy and sell in any city of the world, but also communicate with those from other people groups for the first time since the tower of Babel. After the Hebrew Scriptures were translated into Greek, both Jews and Gentiles had a Bible to prepare them to receive what was about to come.

Significantly, the Roman period created a short period of peace in the empire, thus creating a time when it was safe to travel. With the creation of what would be called the *Pax Romana*, the peace of Rome, there was a guarantee of safe travel for any Roman citizen on Roman roads. Here, then, is how the plan comes together. God was going to call and anoint with the power of the Holy Spirit a Pharisaical Jew from the Diaspora who was born a Roman citizen and fluent in Greek. It was this man, Paul of Tarsus, whom God would send around the empire with police protection on Roman roads to Jewish synagogues where he would read from a Greek Bible with the word that the Scriptures had been fulfilled—by a Jew from Galilee. This Jew, Jesus, had been crucified for the sins of humanity, but had now risen from the dead and ruled the universe from God's right hand. He was calling all men to repentance and new life by the Spirit of God, through whom God would breathe the field manual onto the human heart. No longer would sin rule, because in Christ God had thrown sin as far as the east is from the west. He was now accepting anyone who would come, as is, Jew or Gentile. And so the world was prepared. When the time had fully come, God sent his son....

The Gospels

The Birth of the Christ

Probably sometime in the early winter, AD 30, God's Spirit overshadowed a young, Jewish virgin named Mary and she became pregnant with a male child, THE male child that the biblical story has all along anticipated. It would be this child who would crush the head of the serpent, but would also have his heel bruised. Mary was instructed to name the child *Jesus,* because it was he that was going to save his people from their sins. According to Jeremiah, this would be in fulfillment of the seventh and final covenant in which the barrier of sin separating humankind from God would be done away with once and for all. John's gospel says that Jesus was not only with God but *was* God. What kind of God is this? He was the God who became flesh and dwelt (the Greek word means "to tabernacle") among us. From the perspective of theology, in the event of human rebellion the Trinitarian God had organized a rescue mission before the dawn of time in which the Son of God would become a Son of Man. He would recapitulate Adam so he could pay for the sins of all humankind; Jeremiah said that he would remember our sins no more.

In both Matthew and Luke's genealogies, it is evident that God's plan from the beginning had been to rescue all peoples from their sins. Matthew's list includes Gentiles in Jesus' lineage. David's own grandmother, Ruth, was from Moab. While Matthew's genealogy traces the line back to Abraham, it is Luke's gospel that traces Jesus' heritage all the way back to Adam. God had chosen the Jews, not only to be the people out of whom God would bring the sin-bearer, but also to be the missionary people for the world. It is for this reason that Matthew includes the story of the Magi from the east pursuing whatever prophetic revelation God had given the seekers among their people—and this revelation had led them straight to the Jews. They would have the answer...and so they did. When they found the child, Jesus, they offered him gold, the gift of kings; incense, a gift signifying a new relationship with God; and myrrh, an embalming spice foreshadowing how the King would redeem humankind through his own, sacrificial and substitutionary death.

The Galilee Jesus

It is Mark's gospel that connects us quickly to the Old Testament story by quoting from Isaiah 40 that God would raise up a voice crying in the wilderness to prepare the way for the Lord. John the Baptist, the Elijah of Malachi's prophecy, announced that the Day of the Lord had arrived with the advent of the Christ, Isaiah's anointed one. John said that he was the "Lamb of God who would take away the sin of the world." It was time to repent and believe the good news.

Just as Adam received a blessing prior to receiving his marching orders, Jesus, too, received a blessing at the beginning of his mission. Mark tells us that at his baptism the heavens were torn apart, thus indicating that a new era in redemptive history had begun, and God said, "You are my Son, whom I love; with you I am well pleased." In these two statements God was saying that in Jesus both the vertical ("you is my beloved son") and horizontal ("with you I am well pleased") dimensions that had been ruptured in the Garden had been repaired. He then received the blessing as the Holy Spirit descended on him in the form of a dove, a symbol denoting new creation. One wonders if Jesus would now fulfill Adam's three assignments: to multiply, fill, and rule. And, indeed, that is exactly what he did. Jesus had in his sights nothing less than the glory of God's name being made known through image-bearing disciples that he would raise up from the seed of Abraham, the one who had been blessed to be a blessing to all the peoples of the earth.

After Jesus' anointing for ministry, Mark's gospel shows Jesus immediately choosing disciples so he could multiply God's image within them. Interestingly, he chose most of his twelve disciples from Galilee, a racially mixed area in northern Israel. This is also the area where he was raised and inaugurated his ministry. Given Mark's intentional connection in his gospel to Isaiah's prophesies, it is not surprising to find that it would be Galilee of the Gentiles that would launch Jesus' ministry. A people walking in darkness would see a great light (Is 9.2). Galilee was a racially mixed area and was the perfect launching pad for the one who would be the King over all peoples. It would function as a snapshot of the Jews fulfilling their missionary calling.

Mark also shows Jesus identifying the real enemy when he encounters a demonized man in a synagogue in Galilee. The enemy this time was not Pharaoh, nor Goliath, nor Nebuchadnezzar, nor Antiochus, nor the current antagonist, Rome. No, it was *Satan*. With a word, Jesus cast out the demon with authority. The future image-bearers were watching. This would soon be a part of their ministry as the Eden Project expanded through their words of authority around the world.

Luke also chooses to begin Jesus' public ministry with a pivotal story illustrating God's heart for the world. Jesus had already garnered considerable fame in Galilee when he was invited to address his "home church" in the little Galilean village of Nazareth where he grew up. The scroll on the lectern that day happened to be the one written by Isaiah. Jesus opened it to the section we would call today "Isaiah 61" and began to read that the anointing of the Spirit had come upon *him* (italics mine) and that he, Jesus, was the one about whom Isaiah had prophesied who would proclaim liberty to the captives, give sight to the blind, and proclaim the year of the Lord's favor.

They all marveled at Jesus' words until he pointed out that it had not been the Jews that had received mercy from God in the days of the great prophets, Elijah and Elisha. No, it was a widow from Sidon that Elijah had helped during a time of famine. Moreover, there were many lepers in Israel during the time of Elisha, but it was only Namaan, a Syrian, that received a healing from the Lord. At the mention of Gentiles receiving God's unmerited favor and not Jews, the people Jesus had grown up with suddenly turned on him, thus exposing the same racial prejudice typified in these stories. In the end, it was God's people who were engaged in building the Asphalt Project and not extending to the borders of Eden.

As it touches the Old Testament, then, this foreboding event foreshadows a tragic turn in the story. All along the reader has been aware that God's people could reject her missionary calling because of the sin latent in each nation that was scattered at Babel. But because it was not yet his time to suffer, Jesus passed right through his pack of snarling neighbors who were threatening to throw him off a cliff. The Eden Project would advance with or without ethnic Israel now that the obedient Israelite had arrived. He now went about the business of reconstituting the true Israel around himself. To those who had ears to hear, he gave the kingdom of God.

The term "kingdom of God" was a Jewish code term. They understood it to mean that time when God would return to Israel, forgive their sins, cleanse the temple, defeat her enemies, and restore the Jews to her Davidic glory. Jewish missionaries would call the nations to come to Zion to find God (and, as we shall find out in Acts, the Jews assumed that this meant that the Gentiles would become Jewish). Jesus, however, redefined the entire meaning of the term. When he called people to repentance because the "kingdom of God was at hand," he meant that in his ministry the rule of God had returned to the realm of the earth. No longer did Satan have the upper hand. In and through *his* ministry, Isaiah's prophecy from Isaiah 61 was coming to pass: the year of the

Lord's favor was dawning and was for all who put their trust in him. He, not the temple, was the locus of the forgiveness of sins. In doing so, Jesus was not only King but also Priest of the new Israel, thus fulfilling the types of Adam and David. Moreover, he was now reserving the right to define the members of the new Israel and offering the kingdom of God to all the wrong people apart from the temple's system of forgiveness on his own authority. In the mind of the Jews, even one of these things were enough to get Jesus killed as a false prophet.

In a short parable, Jesus said that the kingdom of God was like plundering a strong man's house. Once the strong man had been tied up, then his goods could be plundered. The meaning of the parable is that even though Satan had violated the people of the earth and had plundered their goods, Jesus had come to bind him up and plunder his house. By forgiving sins, healing every kind of disease and sickness, and freeing the demonized, he was returning to people what had been stolen from them.

Luke describes this process in his account of the healing of a paralyzed man who was lowered down through the roof of a house by some friends into the very room where Jesus was ministering. Luke tells us that the power of the Lord was present that day to heal the sick, thus indicating Jesus' submission as a man to the voice of the Spirit during his earthly ministry (he didn't heal the sick out of his deity but as a human being operating by the power of the Spirit, thus leaving his followers a model to follow in the future). Through the Spirit (Paul would later call these various operations of the Spirit "spiritual gifts"), Jesus discerned that the man needed to know that he was forgiven of his sins so, as the great High Priest, Jesus forgave him of his wrongs (one might surmise that Jesus understood by the Spirit that in this particular case the man's need for forgiveness lay at the heart of his paralytic condition). Immediately, the Jewish leaders in attendance began to judge Jesus in their hearts for the "blasphemy" of presuming to operate as a priest, but Jesus knew what they were thinking (again by the Spirit) and called them on it. Probably operating in what Paul later called the gifts of faith and healing, Jesus told the man to get up and walk. His legs suddenly had life again because the strong man had been bound and Jesus had given back to this man that which the enemy had stolen.

There was a caveat to all this, however. In John's account of Jesus' visit to a pool where the infirmed gathered, he only stopped to heal one man. Jesus would explain these kinds of anomalies saying that he only did what he saw the Father doing. In another illustration of the kingdom's apparent failure to break in, John the Baptist, whom Jesus said was the greatest man who had ever lived, had been arrested and was suffering in prison. "How could the kingdom have come?" he wondered. If anyone would have been worthy to receive the year of the Lord's favor, would it not have been John? Strangely, Jesus himself taught the disciples that the kingdom was a gift, not something earned. Furthermore, if they wanted to see the kingdom come, they would need to invite it to come through prayer, as if they were still waiting for it in some way.

As we gather this seemingly discordant data together, our only conclusion is that while Jesus had inaugurated the end of the age (how else would one account for all Jesus' miracles and the changed lives of people?), the full consummation of the kingdom was still to come. Only at Jesus' return would all tears be dried and the shroud of sin and death over the peoples be completely removed (Is 25.7; Rom 8.20-21). It appears that Jesus' followers live "in-between the times," an era in human history when the kingdom is breaking in all around us, but not in every prayer exchange. We live in an age when the kingdom "now" is overlapped with the kingdom "not yet." This, therefore, is an age of war when we battle in prayer over the lives of people. All can be saved, but not all will be healed and delivered. The poor, Jesus said, will always be with us in this present age. The true kingdom perspective is that if it doesn't break in through our prayers today, we will show up tomorrow, undeterred, undaunted, because Jesus said, "The kingdom of God is at hand." It could break in at any moment. Authentic followers of Jesus, then, have both a *theology of power* and a *theology of pain*; they know why it *does* happen and why, sometimes, it *doesn't*. They are the immovable, unshakable ones who continually pray that the kingdom would come on earth as it is in heaven.

Having laid down the basic lessons of the kingdom of God, it was now time for Jesus to show his disciples the global scope of the kingdom activities that would be entrusted to them. John records an incident where Jesus had the audacity to walk through the region of Samaria on the way back to Galilee from Judea. The Jews hated the Samaritans as the lowest of the low, because after Assyria had scattered the ten Northern tribes in 722 BC, the rabble left in the land, up in Samaria, intermarried with Gentiles, and crafted a religion that was part Jewish and part pagan. Stopping at a well, Jesus sent the disciples ahead to get food. While there, Jesus encountered a woman from Samaria who was apparently barren, because Jesus knew, presumably by the Spirit, that she had had a number of husbands who were no doubt trying to impregnate her to remove her horrible cultural shame. Jesus' supernatural insight into her life, combined with his acceptance of her, as a Jew, broke through her pain. When Jesus told her where to find living water that would quench her thirst forever, she ran back into the village to invite her social network to meet this incredible man. Could he be "the Christ?" she wondered.

Both Mark and Luke record the incident when the disciples have their first cross-cultural experience in the Synoptic gospels. Jesus told the twelve to go to the east side of the Sea of Galilee, an area with ten Gentile cities known as the Decapolis. The disciples no doubt wondered what they were doing *there*. From a cosmic standpoint, this would have appeared to be a bad move. Here, in one small boat, sat the future of the human race. It is not surprising, then, that a storm hit them like a hurricane. Jesus was asleep in the stern, at rest in the rest that God had rested in since the seventh day of creation. He was awakened to the disciple's panic, got up, and rebuked the storm, probably meaning the demonic entities behind the natural phenomena. Suddenly, it was very still. One wonders if the disciples were connecting with how Jesus had cast out demons on other occasions. Very soon they found themselves on the eastern shore in the middle of the night, only to be met by a completely demonized man that had been exiled to a remote beach in chains because no jail could hold him. Again, with the spoken word, Jesus set this man free. Probably a Gentile, he appears to typologically represent the demonized nations in the story. The point is clear: though Jesus has prophetically reconstituted Israel, Satan was not giving up the Gentiles without a fight, but not even Satan could stop the advance of God's kingdom to reach every people group with the gospel. Jesus had cast a demon out of a Jew representing demonized Israel and now a Gentile representing the demonized people groups. Satan's Asphalt Project was going down and the Garden of God would now be filling the earth. The Eden Project had just been thrust into hyperspace.

Jesus' ministry was filled with opportunities for the disciples to see the year of the Lord's favor come to the Gentiles as he prepared them for their apostolic call. Matthew records an incident where a Roman Centurion who believed in the God of the Jews approached Jesus about healing his sick servant. The Roman, however, did not consider himself worthy to have Jesus come to his house, so asked that he just heal him from a distance. Jesus saw in this Gentile's faith a picture of other Gentiles that would come from around the world to eat at Abraham's table. Unfortunately, the Jews would miss the party, ironically because of their racial prejudice and their refusal to accept Jesus' redefinition of the kingdom of God. The Jew's racism is highlighted in a number of gracious encounters that Jesus had with Samaritans. We have already mentioned his dialogue with the woman at the well. He also told a parable of the Good Samaritan where only the man from Samaria bound up the wounds of the traveler that was beaten. Once again, the Jews wallowed in their spirit of elitism. And of the ten lepers that Jesus healed, it was only the Samaritan that returned to thank him.

When Jesus sent out his twelve followers to proclaim the kingdom in Israel and to heal the sick and cast out demons, they came back with a great report that the kingdom had come wherever they had gone in Israel. Luke records that shortly after that Jesus sent out seventy on a similar mission. The number seventy appears to be symbolic of the seventy nations listed in Genesis 10 that grew out of the three sons of Noah. Jesus' seventy kingdom warriors represented those faithful Jews that would, indeed, accept their missionary calling and take the gospel around the world.

The Jerusalem Jesus

As the Galilean phase of his ministry came to a close, Luke records that Jesus "set his face like a flint" to go to Jerusalem to die for the sins of Humankind. It is John's gospel that records the incident that sparked those events. During the late fall of AD 29, Jesus began to stay at the house of Mary, Martha, and Lazarus in Bethany, just two miles from Jerusalem over the Mount of Olives. Throughout the fall and winter of AD 30, Jesus and his disciples went throughout Judea proclaiming the arrival of the kingdom and the Eden Project continued to spread. On one of these excursions, word came to Jesus that Lazarus had become ill. Rather than going back to Bethany immediately, Jesus lingered out among the villages. When he finally did return, he found that Lazarus had died. He had been wrapped and then laid in a tomb that had been sealed with a huge boulder; the funeral was now in full swing. After weeping quietly, Jesus commanded Lazarus to come out of the tomb, which he did, grave clothes and all. News of Lazarus' resurrection precipitated the events that sparked the Passion of the Christ.

Jesus had already predicted three times that he was going to die. He told his disciples that he would be turned over to the Romans, be crucified, and raised on the third day. This was so unbelievable to the disciples that the voice of God spoke to Peter, John, and James once again from the heavens saying, "This is my beloved Son. Listen to him!" Still not getting it, they no doubt joined in the adoring throngs waving palm branches that were symbols of revolt looking back to the time of the violent insurrection of Judas the Maccabee. While riding a donkey, a servant animal destined to carry the burdens of others, Jesus crested the Mt. of Olives with Jerusalem in full view below. The text says that Jesus again wept, this time not the quiet weeping as at Lazarus' tomb, but a loud wailing. At long last, God's glory that Ezekiel had seen in a vision leaving the temple was returning to Israel. Tragically, Israel was missing the hour of God's return to Zion.

Arriving in Jerusalem, Jesus entered the temple as the Messiah was expected to do. After inspecting the temple he returned to Bethany and the next day he and his disciples set out in the morning to go back to Jerusalem. Jesus was hungry and, seeing a fig tree in the distance, hoped to find a few winter figs left on the branches. Upon inspection, he instead found the tree barren. He saw this forlorn tree as a picture of Israel that should have been filled with the best tasting figs of all (i.e., the Gentile nations) but was barren. He cursed the tree and it withered and died. Israel would, indeed, go on to become a barren nation, rejecting and betraying her God by turning his Messiah over to the Romans for trial. The apostle Paul would later write that God had given Israel a "hardening in part until the full number of Gentiles has come in," thus making the Jews jealous of the Gentile harvest (note that the hardening was "in part," meaning that some Jews would believe throughout the history of the Church). When the "times of the Gentiles" had been fulfilled, God would visit Israel again to honor his "irrevocable covenant with Abraham, Isaac and Jacob." He would forgive their sins and "all Israel would be saved" (Rom 11.11ff; cf. Lk 21.24).

Arriving again at the temple, Jesus burned with holy rage. He overturned the money exchange tables and rebuked those that were hawking sacrifices in the outer court of the temple. All three of the Synoptic Gospels record Jesus' quotation of Isaiah 56.7, "My house shall be a house of prayer for all nations." What should have been a missionary prayer meeting had now become a "den of robbers." The tragedy of it all was that the nation that God had redeemed with signs and wonders, and whom he had brought to himself on eagles wings to receive her commission to image God as priests to the nations, had completely missed the entire reason for her existence.

Politically, Jesus was betrayed by Judas, one of the twelve, and was crucified for the crime of insurrection, allegedly claiming to be the king of the Jews and attempting to foment a Maccabean-like rebellion against Pilate. Spiritually, he was the "lamb of God who takes away the sin of the world" (Jn 1.29). Isaiah had seen centuries earlier that though he had done no violence nor had any deceit been in his mouth, Jesus was pierced for *our* transgressions. As our substitute, the Lord laid on him the iniquity of us all and bore the sins of many. John would later write that he was the atoning (Greek, *propitiation*, "appeasing") sacrifice for our sins, and not only for ours but for the sins of the whole world (1 Jn 2.2). In the ninth hour, while darkness covered the earth, Jesus cried out, "My God, my God, why have you forsaken me?" This is the only time in the gospels that Jesus addresses God with his formal name and not the familial term *Father* in Greek (Jesus would have used the Aramaic term, *Abba*). Here he is taking the place of sinful humanity where our sin has prevented us from being family with God—but the sin-bearer paid for sin, broke down the wall and offered those from every nation the inestimable privilege of being adopted into God's family. Only those on the inside can relate to God as their *Abba*.

And again, as Isaiah had seen, the grave couldn't hold him: "after the suffering of his soul he will see the light of life and be satisfied" (Is 53.11). The Bible says that on the third day, just as Jesus had predicted, God raised Jesus from the dead (Acts 13.30) with an imperishable and immortal body as the first fruits of the new creation. The Trinitarian God had, indeed, solved his seemingly impossible dilemma from the Garden of Eden by issuing the death penalty to the Son of Man, the second Adam, and then, through his ability to speak life into being, raised Jesus from the dead, thus showing the Son of Man to also be the Son of God. In doing so, Jesus gave humanity its new start through his life, death, and resurrection by becoming the first fruits of the New Creation. Paul would later say that at the return of Christ to the earth to consumate the kingdom of God, we would all be raised with him and receive our imperishable and immortal bodies to reign with him as part of a renewed earth.

The risen Christ then appeared to his disciples and many others as proof that he was, indeed, Jesus of Nazareth, crucified but now raised from the dead. In private sessions led by the Spirit, he spent the next forty days with his disciples reviewing all his lessons he had taught them about the kingdom of God. As the grand finale, he told them to rendezvous with him back in Galilee where it had all begun. On a mountain, he gave them a commission to disciple all the nations of the earth, *as nations*. They were to find the Asphalt Peoples created by the dispersion of languages at Babel and expand Eden into any asphalt cracks they could find. They were to baptize (immerse) people into the name of the Triune God and teach them to obey every lesson he had taught them about the kingdom. And, most importantly, Jesus said that he would be *with them* as they fanned out around the globe in fulfillment of the promise to Abraham that his seed would carry a blessing for all the tribes of the earth. To carry out their mission, however, they would need a blessing such as had been given to Adam, to all the great leaders of the Old Testament, and then to Jesus himself. Luke's gospel ends, therefore, with Jesus telling the disciples that they should wait in Jerusalem for the empowerment of the Holy Spirit. From there, they would preach the kingdom of God to all nations, beginning in Jerusalem. When the job was done, the end would come (Mt 24.14; Lk 24.47). With that

Jesus ascended into heaven. When the mission to the nations was completed, he would return in the clouds, exactly as he had left.

The Story of the Early Church

Among the gospel writers, only Luke intended to add a "part two" to his account of the life of Jesus of Nazareth. The book of Acts, therefore, begins with Luke explaining that in his former book, the gospel of Luke, he wrote about all that Jesus *began* to do and teach. The inference is that Acts—and all of church history for that matter—is going to be about what Jesus will *continue* to do and teach, but now through the lives of his disciples. After reviewing all that he had taught them about the kingdom of God, Jesus told them to wait in Jerusalem for the promised Holy Spirit and then ascended into heaven. Only as the ascended Christ, the one seated in the position of absolute authority at God's right hand, would Jesus then have the authority to pour out the Spirit to empower the church for her worldwide mission to expand the Eden Project. It would begin in Jerusalem and then expand in waves until it reached the "uttermost parts of the earth" when all people groups had received Abram's blessing. Luke appears to have structured Acts, then, around a series of cross-cultural waves of the gospel, beginning with mainstream Judaism, and then moving outward to fringe Judaism. From there, it would progress into the Gentile world penetrating Syria, then Asia, and then Europe. Acts ends with the apostle Paul alive in Rome, the center of the empire, and teaching about the kingdom of God and Jesus as the Christ. Luke is telling his readers that the gospel will continue to move forward unhindered until the global mission of the church is complete and the ascended Christ returns.

And so, on the day of Pentecost, the day when the tithe

of the harvest was brought to the temple in Jerusalem, the Spirit fell on one hundred twenty disciples to empower them for their worldwide mission. The Spirit manifest as tongues of fire and each one spoke in another language as the Spirit enabled them, thus fulfilling Joel's prediction that in the last days, God would pour out the Spirit of prophecy. Intimate, two-way communication with God was available universally for the first time since the Garden. Full of the Spirit, the disciples then went out into the streets praising God in their new languages. In a clear fulfillment of the strategy of God with the dispersion of languages at Babel, men and women from the Diaspora heard them praising God in their native tongues. At the preaching of Peter, three thousand people were converted to Christ as the tithe of the end-time harvest and each Jew went back to their native countries to share what Christ had done. Despite the fact that most of the Jews were like barren fig trees with nothing to offer, those Jews that had ears to hear had the joy of fulfilling their commission to be a kingdom of priests and a holy nation (Ex 19.6).

From here, Luke chronicles the advance of the Eden Project against an array of obstacles. In the first wave to mainstream Judaism, we read of two arrests of the early believers by Jewish authorities, tragically the newest members of the Asphalt Project. In the first case, the arrest of Peter and John for healing a man lame from birth only emboldened the believers in prayer and witness. The two apostles were then released. In the second case, the arrest of all the apostles, an angel released them to continue to preach. The jails of men could not hold back the gospel...but what about sin in the camp?

Luke now tells the story of two believers, a couple named Ananias and Sapphira, who lied about the price of a piece of land they had sold to donate to the church because they had held some money back for themselves. Peter, full of the Spirit, saw right through it and each dropped dead in turn. The text says that from that time on, the fear of the Lord filled Jerusalem; everyone—believer and unbeliever alike—realized that gathering in the Lord's presence was serious business.

In the final episode of the first wave of the gospel to mainstream Judaism, Luke chronicles the potential of racial prejudice to thwart the kingdom's progress. There were many poor widows in Jerusalem at that time and quite a number of them had become believers in Jesus. The church responded by starting a food ministry to care for them, but the Aramaic-speaking widows native to Israel were being preferred over those that had come from the Diaspora and spoke Greek. While it appears that this was Satan's attempt to divide the church over racial lines, the Holy Spirit directed the apostles to appoint seven Greek-speaking men to oversee the food distribution. What could have been a split became the first opportunity to multiply cross-cultural leadership. Not only was the crisis averted, but also the appointment of this new leadership looks forward to the missionary movement that was just over the horizon.

The second wave of the gospel to fringe Judaism in Judea and Samaria begins with the arrest of Stephen, one of the seven. It appears that his food pantry ministry had expanded into a ministry in evangelism accompanied by great signs and wonders. He also is the first one recorded that understood that Christianity and Judaism were incompatible in regard to both the temple (Jesus' once-for-all sacrifice had rendered the temple obsolete) and the law (Jeremiah said that God would write the law on our minds and hearts). He was arrested for his teaching and put on trial before the Jewish ruling council. In his defense, Stephen accused the Jewish leaders of being in alignment with those Jewish leaders in Israel's history that had continually rejected the prophets. He was right. Now ironically playing the part of the enemies of Israel, the Jewish leaders took Stephen outside the city gates and stoned him as the first martyr of the Christian Church. As they did so, they laid their coats at the feet of a young rabbi named Saul, from Tarsus in Asia Minor. In this way Luke subtly introduces the man who would become the next great character in the story.

What could have been a fatal blow, however, turned out to be the flashpoint for the cross-cultural transmission of the gospel by the seed of Abram. A persecution broke out by the Jews, apparently against the Greek-speaking element in the church. Another one of the seven, Philip, was sent to Samaria where he preached the gospel of the kingdom accompanied by great signs. This appears to be a demonic stronghold, because many demons were cast out and we encounter the first sorcerer in the story, a man named Simon. When Peter and John are sent from Jerusalem to inspect Philip's ministry, the Holy Spirit fell on the Samaritans just as he had fallen on the Jews. The importance of this event is twofold. First, Luke sees the Samaritans as the representatives of the ten northern tribes that had been scattered by the Assyrians. Israel's mission to the Gentiles could not commence until the "ten lost tribes" had been reunited with the two tribes from Judah that had come back to Israel at the end of their Babylonian exile. Even though the bulk of the task of restoring the ten tribes lay yet in the future, the ingathering of the Samaritans was a picture of that which was to come as God's missionary people went from people to people winning pockets of scattered Jews to Christ. Second, God here accepts the Samaritans as they are without their having to become Jews first. Grace such as this would have never crossed a Jew's mind, not even the minds of Peter and John who laid hands on them to receive the Holy Spirit as the Jews had. With this, both Peter and John preached in Samaritan villages on their way back to Jerusalem

Meanwhile, an angel sent Philip to a desert road leading south. There he encountered a man riding in a chariot who just happened to be the treasurer who served the Queen of Ethiopia. The man was a Gentile that worshiped the God of the Jews and happened to be reading from the scroll of Isaiah when Philip pulled up alongside his chariot. When Philip explained that Isaiah's prophecy had been fulfilled in Jesus, the Christ, the eunuch was converted and baptized on the spot. While we have no information in church history about whatever happened to this influential man, it is clear that this is Luke's way of telling his readers that the gospel was being transmitted from a Greek-speaking Jew to a black African who would then take the gospel back to North Africa.

At this point Luke reconnects us with the young rabbi that had been introduced earlier named Saul. He was a Greek-speaking Diaspora Jew from Tarsus in Asia Minor who also happened to be born a Roman citizen. He had been sent as a Jewish emissary to Damascus to arrest followers of Jesus, but on the road was apprehended by a light so bright that it blinded him and he fell to the ground. It was here that the risen Christ appeared to him and informed him that he was the one appointed to bring the gospel to the Gentiles. Saul was then taken into Damascus where his blindness was healed and he was filled with the Holy Spirit. He immediately began to preach in Damascus that he had been wrong about Jesus and that he was, indeed, the Christ who had been crucified and had been raised to the right hand of God. Persecution broke out against Saul, and after narrowly escaping Damascus, he went to Jerusalem where a man named Joseph, nicknamed Barnabas meaning "son of encouragement," vouched for his integrity before the apostles. He preached freely in Jerusalem until debates with Grecian Jews sparked persecution against him there and he escaped once again, this time back to Tarsus. He will reemerge later in the story, but now Luke reconnects his readers with the ministry of Peter.

After giving accounts of Peter healing a paralytic and raising a young girl from the dead, Luke zeroes in on a Roman Centurion living in Caesarea who was a follower of the God of the Jews. An angel appeared to him and told him that God had seen his devotion and his generous giving to the poor. He was to send for a man named Peter, who was staying in Joppa, thirty miles to the south. This man had a message that Cornelius needed to hear. Messengers were immediately dispatched. Meanwhile, Peter had been staying at the house of Simon, the tanner (considered an "unclean" profession by the Jews), and was on his roof praying. Suddenly he had a vision of a sheet being lowered down from heaven filled with unclean animals. God told Peter to kill the animals and eat them but Peter was appalled at the thought. As a Jew, he had never eaten anything but kosher food. The vision happened not once, not twice, but *three* times. Was Peter getting the point? God was declaring that what was formerly unclean was now clean. At that, there was a knock on the door and Gentile servants sent from Cornelius invited Peter to travel with them to the north to see their master. It was now clear to Peter that God was up to something, so he resolutely set off with the messengers.

Upon arriving in Caesarea, Peter would no doubt have been surprised to find that Cornelius had gathered his entire social network—of Gentiles. As Peter stood at the threshold of Cornelius' home, the entire story of God hung in the balance. Would Peter literally *step* into his role as the seed of Abram and bless the Gentiles? Praise the Lord. He did—and it would appear that the ascended Christ was so excited about this moment that as Peter began to preach, the Spirit was poured out upon the Gentiles and they too received the ability to prophesy, just as the Jews (and seemingly the Samaritans) had. With the conversion, filling, and baptism of the Gentiles, Luke has shown that God wants to save and empower all people with the Holy Spirit and incorporate them into the family of God.

A lingering question remains, however, and here we are taken right back to Stephen's inflammatory assertions that the temple and the law were no longer needed. While it was clear now that the temple had been rendered obsolete by the atoning death of Christ, the Gentile's relationship to the law and to boundary markers like circumcision and food laws was anything but resolved in the minds of some. This issue would soon come to a head because events were about to transpire that would radically shift the culture of the church.

The gospel's transmission to the Gentiles was initiated once again by the Holy Spirit. A church had been started in Antioch in Syria by a multi-cultural missionary team from the island of Cyprus and Cyrene in North Africa. There was such a move of the Spirit in Antioch through these missionaries that Barnabas was sent down from Jerusalem to oversee the work. Quickly sensing that he would need help, Barnabas remembered his friendship with Saul of Tarsus from many years earlier. Barnabas went to Tarsus, found Saul, and persuaded him to come back to help him mature the work in Antioch. Later, as the teachers and prophets of the church were fasting and seeking the Lord, the Holy Spirit spoke prophetically telling them to set apart Barnabas and Saul for the work to which they had been called. After fasting they laid hands on the two men and commissioned them off on what we now call the "first missionary journey" to expand the Eden Project in Asia Minor.

Their first stop was on Barnabas' home island of Cyprus. There they met a Jewish sorcerer who challenged their authority. The power of God fell on Saul, now referred to by his Greek name, Paul, and the sorcerer was struck blind. From this time on, the leadership dynamic on the team shifts to Paul as Luke subtly changes the order of their names to "Paul and Barnabas." After arriving in Asia Minor, Paul and Barnabas extend their missionary work into a series of Greek cities in Asia Minor including Pisidia, Iconium, Lystra, and Derbe. In Pisidia, we find the pattern that Paul will follow in every city in which he preaches the gospel. After arriving, Paul would network with local Jews, and, as a visiting rabbi, was generally invited to address a synagogue service. There he preached that Jesus had been crucified, but that God had vindicated him by raising him from the dead. He then invited people to become baptized and Spirit-filled followers of Jesus. Also, as a general rule, some Jews believed, but most did not. Paul was then forced to wipe the dust off his shoes and turn to the Gentile harvest. Very quickly the church in the Diaspora became predominantly Gentile, thus creating the cultural problems mentioned earlier. This pattern, "to the Jew first, then the Greek" (Rom 2.10), was the outworking of God's original plan:

- Breaking the world up into language groups to scatter them around the globe
- Picking one man, Abram, and giving him and his seed a commission as God's people for the world
- Scattering this people throughout the world at the hand of Assyria
- Unifying the world under one language, Greek

- Translating the Jewish Scriptures into Greek
- Using Rome to bring the *Pax Romana*, establishing peace, connecting the empire with roads, and guaranteeing police protection for Roman citizens

Once again we see that when the time had fully come, God sent his son (Gal 4.4). Captalizing on the timing, God raised up a Jewish citizen from the Roman Diaspora, fluent in both Aramaic and Greek, and trained as a rabbi to be the spostle to the Gentiles. Paul would later introduce his letter to the church at Rome with a clear statement of the apostolic mission:

> Through him and for his name's sake, we received grace and apostleship to call people from among all the Gentiles to the obedience that comes from faith (Rom 1.5).

Paul's increasingly Gentile churches were not required to keep the law, thus precipitating a highly volatile church council. In attendance were those apostles who could be present along with members from two groups, (1) the Jewish-Christian leaders that believed that Gentiles had to become Jewish in order to become full followers of Jesus and (2) Paul and his contingent that accepted Gentile peoples *as peoples* and did not require them to adopt Jewish laws or customs. Paul did not need the blessing of the leaders in Jerusalem; because he had received his commission and his gospel from the risen Christ (Gal 1.11). He did, however, desire it for the sake of unity. In the end, the day belonged to Peter as he reiterated that it was God himself who had poured out the Holy Spirit on the Samaritans and the Gentiles without requiring them to keep the law first. James, the brother of Jesus and now the leader of the church in Jerusalem, then blessed the Pauline (law-free) gospel, only asking that Gentile converts be sensitive to Jewish cultural issues to preserve unity. This Paul was glad to do.

The rest of the book of Acts chronicles Paul's apostolic exploits to fulfill Jesus' prophetic word that the gospel would move cross-culturally from Jerusalem, through Judea and Samaria, Syria, Asia, and then Europe. Interestingly, Paul's second missionary journey began with what appeared to be a tragic rupture in the leadership team. In a heated disagreement over whether to take a young missionary named John Mark, Barnabas left with Mark, never to be heard from in Acts again. Paul, however, set off with a prophet named Silas to revisit the churches from the first journey. After repeated attempts to take the word of the Lord east, Luke tells us that they were "prevented by the Holy Spirit" from going into Asia. As they regrouped in the seaport town of Troas, Paul had a dream of a man from Greece who motioned for him to go west, not east. This is another hinge point in the history of the world. The gospel would take root on European soil with its high value for reading and writing. This would serve to disseminate papyri of the New Testament, thus giving doctrinal objectivity and direction to the churches. The east, however, with its value on oral culture, was not successfully evangelized and the Bible was not valued in the same manner as in the west. On this part of the second missionary thrust, churches were successfully planted throughout Greece despite severe attacks of the Jews, and a near run-in with the Roman state in the city of Corinth.

Paul's third missionary journey saw him plant a great church in the Aegean seaport city of Ephesus in Asia Minor. This work was characterized by unusual demonstrations of the Spirit's power and freed many from idolatry and demons. Not even Jewish exorcists and the great cult of Artemis, the Greek name for the Roman god Diana, could stop the word of the Lord. The word of God was so powerful that Luke tells us that, "all the Jews and Greeks in the province of

Asia heard the word of the Lord." Luke sums up this wave of the gospel to the Gentiles in Europe commenting on the signs and wonders that accompanied the proclamation of the kingdom and the Christ. He says, "In this way the word of the Lord spread widely and grew in power."

At this phase of Paul's life, he was convinced that the Lord wanted him to go to Jerusalem as a witness. It had been prophesied that he would be arrested there and in all likelihood he would be killed. But, like Jesus, Paul set his face like a flint to go to Jerusalem, the city where prophets went to die. After arriving, he was recognized by the Jews when he entered the temple and a riot ensued. But for the swift work of Roman soldiers he, too, would have met his death there, but God had other intentions.

After being saved from the ravenous Jews, Paul spent the next few years in various Roman prisons awaiting trial. Becasue the case against Paul was so weak, he would have been freed if he had not appealed his case to the highest court in Rome. Luke's last scenes follow Paul's journey by ship to Rome. Even then the enemy tried to kill him. Weathering storms, a shipwreck and a snakebite, Paul was led by Roman guard into the very center of the Roman Empire. After Paul arrived, he met with the Jewish leaders. Becasue they were unfamiliar with Paul's case, Luke uses the incident to cement the fact that the Jewish rejection of the gospel was not based on any kind of localism. It was, rather, something God had done. When he shared the good news with them, the reader encounters the Jew's typical response: a few believed but most rejected. As was his pattern, Paul turned to the Gentiles upon Jewish rejection and preached the good news of Jesus as the Jewish Messiah and the dawn of the kingdom of God through him. By ending Acts in chapter 28 with Paul alive in the center of the Empire, Luke is saying that the message of

Christ and his kingdom would be preached to the uttermost parts of the earth. There would be a chapter 29, and 30, and so forth, all the way to the end of the age when the times of the Gentiles will have reached its fulfillment.

The Finale

While a full rendition of the biblical data of the end of the age lies far beyond this short story, I want to point out a number of biblical motifs that find their fulfillment in the book of Revelation. First, God's plan to break the world into different languages in a divide-to-reach strategy must be vindicated before Christ returns. The world mission of the church will come to completion. John saw it clearly in Revelation 7.9:

> After this I looked and there before me was a great multitude that no one could count, from every nation, tribe, people and language, standing before the throne and in front of the Lamb. They were wearing white robes and were holding palm branches in their hands. And they cried out in a loud voice:
>
> "Salvation belongs to our God,
> who sits on the throne,
> and to the Lamb."

Second, as with a woman in labor, the Eden Project must be finished during times of great suffering. These times of suffering will culminate in a period of great tribulation unlike any the world has ever seen, nor ever will again. During that time, the Asphalt Project will vomit out a time of unprecedented martyrdom for those that have the courage and faith to stand up against the Antichrist. But, in God's final triumph, Babylon the Great, John's metaphor for Rome and Satan's system of evil, will be defeated in a single day. While the people of the Asphalt Project are declaring peace and safety, destruction will come on them suddenly. It will be as in the days of Noah when God shut his people in the ark and those who mocked Noah died in an outpouring of the wrath of God when he returned the earth to its beginnings to establish a new creation. It will be as it was in the days of Moses when God's angel of death passed over his people and saved a remnant for himself before throwing Pharaoh's horse and rider into the sea. So too the Antichrist's forces will be destroyed and Satan and his demons will be locked up, thus removing the shroud of death from the earth. That, for which the created order groaned, will come.

Third, when the gospel of the kingdom has been preached as a witness to every nation and the Gentile mission comes to completion, Christ will return in his resurrected body to the earth. Just when it will appear that the forces of the Antichrist will annihilate the people of God in a final battle between light and dark, Jesus will come back riding a white horse. On his thigh will be written, KING OF KINGS AND LORD OF LORDS. With one swing of his sword, Satan will be defeated.

Fourth, it is likely that at the return of Christ, there will be a massive harvest among ethnic Jews. Zechariah saw that a day was coming when the Lord would lift the blindness over the Jews and give them grace to humble themselves and pray. They will suddenly recognize Jesus as the one they had pierced at the cross and will mourn for him as a mother mourns for a child. Paul said that it would be at this time when all Israel, men and women from all twelve tribes, would be saved.

Fifth, Paul told his churches that it was at this time when all the believers that had ever lived would rise to meet Christ in the air—the true time of the rapture—and so we will be with the Lord forever.

Sixth, with Satan bound, it is likely that the earth will now enjoy a time of peace when all that God had purposed in the Eden Project will come to fulfillment. In the ultimate fulfillment of Solomon's table and kingdom in 1 Kings 4, the kingdom of God would come to the earth so thoroughly that the knowledge of the glory of the Lord would cover the earth as the waters cover the sea. It is this time that Peter prophesied about when he said that a time was coming when God would restore everything by bringing to pass all that the prophets had foreseen. The lion will dwell with the lamb and like a child he will lead them.

Seventh, John saw that at the end of this period of restoration, Satan will be released for one, final time of rebellion. He will deceive the nations, that Daniel and John call Gog and Magog, into rebellion against the Christ, but they will be thrown into the lake of fire, never to rise again.

Eighth, it is at this point that what Daniel had seen would come to pass. Another resurrection from the dead must take place where all those who had been a part of the Asphalt Project will rise. Now, standing before the great white throne of God almighty will be every human being that had ever lived. Books will be opened in which are written the thoughts and deeds of every man, woman, boy, and girl. All will be found wanting before the Holy God. Thank the Lord, however, for there are other books. In these books are written the names of all those who have trusted in the blood of Jesus. Those from the Asphalt Project that have rejected Christ will be found wanting and will be thrown into what John calls "the lake of fire." All those who have trusted Christ will be welcomed into eternal life.

Ninth, there will now commence what John calls the Wedding Supper of the Lamb. Christ, the bridegroom, would redeem a bride without spot or wrinkle from every nation. She will be dressed in white linen, representing the righteous acts of the saints. Awards will then be given. Those who have lived their Christian lives well, investing their talents and building with what Paul calls gold, silver, and precious stones, will hear the words, "Well done my good and faithful servant." They will be given awards that neither moth nor rust can destroy. Those who have built with wood, hay, and stubble, squandering the one thing humans can never get back—time—will be saved, but as it were through fire, with the smell of smoke on their clothes. They will have no rewards.

Finally, in Revelation 21, we see the Eden Project coming to its final fulfillment. The New Jerusalem, an apocalyptic temple without an inner or outer court, will descend from heaven onto the earth. It will consist only of the Most Holy Place, which is the presence of God. God's kingdom will be Daniel's mountain that will fill the whole earth. John said,

> And I heard a loud voice from the throne saying, "Now the dwelling of God is with men, and he will live with them. They will be his people, and God himself will be with them and be their God. He will wipe every tear from their eyes. There will be no more death or mourning or crying or pain, for the old order of things has passed away." He who was seated on the throne said, "I am making everything new!" (Rev 21.3-5).

As God had declared through the prophet Isaiah, "I will make known the end from the beginning, from ancient times what is still to come. I say my purpose will stand and I will do all that I please (Is 46.10). Nothing is going to stop the Eden Project from being completed and God will receive the glory due his name.

NOW WHAT?

Reading the Bible in Alignment with the Plot

Congratulations! You have finished *The Eden Project*, the Bible as a short story. I hope you were drawn in by the story itself. As you were reading, were you beginning to connect the dots? If so, you're not alone. In the last twenty-plus years, I have told this story to thousands of people. They have told me time and again that seeing God's grand plan for his creation changed their lives. One man told me that he has listened to the DVDs of this presentation seven times, absorbing God's purposes into his being. People are hungry to know how to make sense of the world.

One of the biggest problems in America today is that we have very little sense of history. Without an adequate philosophy of history, we are, as it is said, destined to repeat it. It is my prayer that in this brief exposure to the eternal plan of God, he will meet you and give you a renewed vision for your personal story as one of the sons and daughters of the redeemed Adam. As you have this encounter, I also hope you begin to discover the unique contribution you can make to fulfill God's plan for the world.

This concluding chapter will attempt to show how knowing this narrative has changed the way I understand the Bible and live my life. To demonstrate how my life changed, I will look at two narrative passages, one from the Old Testament and one from the New Testament and use them as models of how to read the Bible as one story. As I read these two smaller stories in light of the bigger story, I believe that you will see them in new ways as I did.

Basic to interpreting the narrative portions of the Scriptures is to reconstruct the historical contexts into which those stories were written. Even the other genres of the Bible, like the letters and the psalms, are written in historical contexts and can come alive to us as we attempt to reconstruct their settings as well. The first key to interpreting biblical stories is to see that they need to be read at three different levels. The first level has to do with what the story means within the book in which it appears. How does this story function in developing the author's purposes in its original setting? Next, we need to ask how the story advances the development of the people of God on the earth. Finally, we need to ask how each story contributes to the cosmic plan of God. This would include all the material in Genesis 1-11 that shows how the world got the way it is. The cosmic plan would speak to things regarding the male child who will crush the serpent's head, Noah and his flood, the tower of Babel, and reaching the nations. God's ultimate desire is to restore the creation originally given to Adam and Eve. God's desire in this effort is to restore two assumptions (vertical and horizontal relationships will be made right) and three assignments (multiply, fill, and rule). Here we could also trace the theme of the blessing of the Holy Spirit, the source of change and power that moves God's people and story forward. Let us now examine an Old and New Testament story to see these interpretive principles in action.

Elijah and the Prophets of Ba'al

One of the most important biblical figures is the prophet Elijah. He is one of only two people in human history that did not experience death. Genesis says that "Enoch walked with God and he was not." The writer of the book of Kings then tells us that Elijah was taken to heaven in a fiery chariot. Talk about an exit. At the end of the Old Testament, the prophet Malachi predicts that Elijah would reappear before the coming of the great and terrible day of the Lord to prepare the way for him. He would turn the hearts of the fathers to the children and the children to the fathers, lest he strike the land with a curse. Later, Jesus would say that John the Baptist was the fulfillment of Malachi's Elijah prophecy and that before the Christian era, of all those who had ever lived, no one was greater than John. If John had enacted the return of Elijah, then it appears that he is a very important figure to study. I will here attempt to show that it is impossible to understand the significance of Elijah without knowing the bigger story of God.

What Does the Story Mean in the Book?

The Elijah narrative is quite long. For our purposes here, we will focus solely on the most famous of Elijah's stories, which was his call to repentance from and victory over the worship of Ba'al and his female counterpart, Asherah, on Mt. Carmel. Together, these gods allegedly controlled fertility, in both humankind and in agriculture. For the ancient, it was Ba'al that sent the rain.

To understand how this story functions in the book of 1 Kings, one must have a thorough grasp of the historical context. Elijah emerges in the ninth century BC, just after civil war broke out under Solomon's son, Rehoboam, king of Judah in the south. About sixty years later, Ahab, son of the prosperous Omri, became king of the northern state of Israel. The Bible story reveals that Ahab repeated the sins of Israel's first king, Jeroboam, "as if it were a trivial thing." But he did not stop there. Early in his reign, he established an ungodly alliance with Syria by marrying Jezebel, a priestess of Ba'al, and built what was called, mysteriously, an Asherah pole. While the specific meaning of the pole is lost to us, it was clearly the cult symbol for the goddess of fertility. If this male and female deity could be induced to have intercourse, it was thought that the rain would come and the land would bear fruit. When there was a drought, the ancients escalated cult prostitution to entice Ba'al and Asherah to increase their intimacy to fertilize the ground. When Ahab made Ba'al worship the national religion, it was a complete rejection of Yahweh as the King of Israel. In this way, the writer of Kings says that Ahab sinned more than any of the kings before him.

As one might expect, God became deeply concerned. He raised up Elijah as the first national prophet to enforce the Deuteronomic Covenant so that his name would not be defamed among the nations. Elijah did not write a book as some of the other prophets did, so we only know of him from the stories in 1 Kings. What he did, however, made him the model for all subsequent prophetic activity.

When God sent a three-year famine, it was the perfect Covenantal curse for those who had stopped trusting God to send the rain. God told Elijah to announce the drought to Ahab. After he did, the Lord sent him into the desert where he drank by the brook, Cherith, and was fed with food brought by ravens. When the brook dried up and the ravens stopped coming, Elijah moved on and visited a Gentile widow in Syria that, in contrast to Israel, trusted Israel's God. He provided for her through Elijah's word of the Lord, which came to him to confront Ahab. He called for a showdown with the prophets of Ba'al and this led to the famous power encounter on Mt. Carmel.

Elijah ordered a sacrifice to be offered and water to be poured on it to make it hard for the sacrifice to be consumed by fire. Those who worshipped Ba'al could not entice him to come down and consume the sacrifice, despite their ardent worship. Elijah's prayer, on the other hand, was received by the Lord and the sacrifice was consumed by fire from heaven. After the slaughter of all the cult leaders, Elijah prayed that God would send rain and remained in this posture until he saw a small cloud on the horizon. He knew that a powerful rain was on its way signaling the end of the drought. This encouraged those who had remained secretly faithful to step forward concerning their faith. The worship of Yahweh received a boost—at least for a while. Jezebel was still the queen and she has the infamous reputation as the most wicked woman in the Bible.

To know how to interpret this story, the reader has to determine how it functions within the book of Kings. The writer is attempting to chronicle the demise of Israel, from the highpoint under Solomon to its two destructions. The ten, northern tribes of Israel were destroyed by Assyria in 722 BC, and the two, southern tribes of Judah by Babylon in 586 BC. Along the way, he points out time and again that Israel's status as a nation at any point is tied to her obedience or disobedience to the Covenant in Deuteronomy.

The story of Mt. Carmel functions in Kings to show that Elijah was the first prophet willing to speak out publically against the hideous Ba'al worship cult that had taken hold of Israel like a plague. He was a man of faith who was willing to live by the hand of the Lord and to confront evil at the expense of his own life. This same tenacity is exactly what John the Baptist had and why Jesus said that John was the fulfillment of Malachi's prophecy about the return of Elijah before the Day of the Lord. Elijah became a pattern for those called to speak out at a national level against sin and to call for a return to God's standards for worship and holy living. In turn, God confirmed Elijah's word with signs and wonders. We can see elements of his faith and action in the prophets that come after him. His life , then, plays a pivotal role in the book of Kings and serves as an example of the kind of things one might be called to do in speaking out against dark forces of injustice and ungodliness.

Advancing the Development of God's People

I worked on a framing crew as we were planting one of our churches. All day long the guys would swear and tell dirty jokes, while heavy metal music blared in the background. To keep my heart from getting affected by this barrage of darkness, I prayed throughout the day to keep my heart tender. The guys knew I was a follower of Jesus because I was very open about my faith. One day, the crew began defaming the name of the Lord by using a profoundly offensive combination of his name with a particular swear word. I prayed, trying to drown it out, but this particular combination of words was so offensive that suddenly I felt the anger of the Lord come upon me. This was not an emotion generating from within me, but one that was given to me so I would know how the Lord felt about his name being defamed. I took my big, steel framing hammer and threw it down on the subfloor so hard, it bounced. I then looked directly at the crew who were now staring at me, and said in strong voice, "I don't ever want to hear you use the Lord's name like that again!" The fear of the Lord fell on them in varying degrees, depending on the state of their hearts, and they never used that phrase again in my hearing.

These events are called power encounters, a direct confrontation with the enemy in God's timing. I have had many of these over the years. They occur when we make kingdom inroads into satanic turf, whether penetrating new ground for the gospel or in someone's life. When we intentionally step into darkness to shine the light, we eventually run into demonic presences of various kinds. When I do, I remind myself of the authority I have been given in Christ to "bind" (say "No!") to these entities and cast them out. A word of caution, however, as we will see in our next passage, let us not become enamored with the authority we have been given to cast out demons, but rejoice that our names are written in heaven.

Now, having seen how this story functions in the book of Kings, what can we learn about the growth of God's people? We first note that this story cannot be understood fully apart from its connection to Deuteronomy 28 with its blessings and curses meted out for obedience or disobedience. One of the covenantal curses listed there is drought. Since Ba'al and Asherah were thought to be the gods that sent rain if worshipped correctly, it is appropriate that God's call to Israel to repent would come in the form of a drought. God held rain back in Israel for three years to produce humility. Perhaps now they would return to the Covenant and set a pattern that the northern tribes could follow. The people of God were at a crossroads. Unfortunately, as the saying goes, a leopard cannot change its spots. To use the language of Paul in the New Testament book of Romans, they suppressed the truth to justify the wicked lifestyle they had chosen.

Ahab and Elijah were two leaders going in opposite directions. Unfortunately, they were on the same team. Both were Israelites, but only Elijah stood for the Covenant and for the forward progress of the people of God according to that Covenant. In terms of role, Ahab was the structural leader and Elijah the prophet called by God to hold him accountable. In my almost forty years pastoring in local churches, I have played both these roles. I have been the structural leader that did not want to listen to my wise counselors and prophets. I have also been a wise counselor and prophetic voice to structural leaders that did not want to receive what I was saying. Once, I played the prophetic role among some structural leaders at a conference. I taught on the kingdom of God and challenged this particular group to embrace hearing the voice of God in the present day. The Lord gave me multiple prophetic words for the group and God began moving powerfully. People began praying for one another and several people began to be healed and empowered for evangelism. The next day the main leaders confronted me in an accusatory way. I was unusually peaceful and stood my ground both biblically and experientially. Just as I was about to be soundly rebuked, one of the most respected among them said that one of his staff had been healed of a significant medical issue. Once it was out in the open, another leader said something similar. The two or three who were leading the charge against my prophetic voice into their culture were suddenly silenced and we finished the conference on good ground.

This was actually a combination of a power encounter at the personal level and the vindication of the prophetic voice at the level of the story of the people of God. In the forward movement of the church, kings will often reject prophetic input. Expect persecution if God puts you in this role. Speak the word of the Lord and expect to be persecuted as Elijah was, as the next parts of the story tell us. Attack and counterattack with prophets and kings; this is the way the people of God often move forward. As an aside, I might also mention to have your heart ready to receive helpful input from structural leaders. Prophetic people need healing, too, and often the way we deliver our message needs to be tempered with wisdom and kindness.

Contributions to the Cosmic Plan of God

How can this passage be understood at the cosmic level of redemption? The main elements of redemptive interpretation include the motifs of sacrificial death and resurrection. In terms of sacrifice, we see several subtextual indicators. First, God received Elijah's sacrifice because it was offered in faith. Just as with Abel, who offered a better sacrifice than Cain by faith, Elijah trusted the God of Israel for rain and offered his sacrifice in the same heart. Despite dramatic worship by the prophets of Ba'al, they found their efforts at religious ritual worthless. In the words of the former prophet, Samuel, to obey is better than sacrifice. Second, Elijah stood as one man for the proper way to deal with national sin: holy sacrifice acceptable to God through a penitent worshipper. Third, in terms of resurrection, we see the faithfulness of Elijah effecting a national resurrection through the ending of the drought. The rains, sent by God as he promised, caused the kingdom of God to flourish. Fourth, we see Elijah turning not to Israel but to the widow from Syria when he needed help. This pattern of most of the Jews rejecting and the Gentiles being receptive to a faithful Jew sets a precedent for a pattern in history. Jesus will encounter this, as will the apostles in Acts.

In all this, we see a picture of Christ, the one who stood for the many; the one who offered a holy and acceptable sacrifice for Israel that was received by God; the one who experienced resurrection life, who sent the rain, and created abundance in the kingdom of God; the one who reached out as a Jew to the other nations with the good news that God accepts all those who receive him by faith.

Luke's Sending of the Seventy

Only in Luke's gospel do we find Jesus sending seventy to prepare his way as he "set his face like a flint" to go to Jerusalem to die. The seventy that were sent probably excludes the twelve, since they had already been sent on a missionary excursion to the Jews (Lk 9). Luke is the only Gentile writer in the New Testament and it makes sense that he would want to show an account foreshadowing the call on Israel to be the missionary people for the world. The choice of Jesus to choose seventy is based on the meaning of "seventy." It could refer to the seventy elders of Israel, but it is more likely that it is a reference to the seventy nations that came from the sons of Noah that are listed in Genesis 10. As such, the seventy in Luke's gospel could be understood as a prophetic picture of Israel's missionary purpose. After giving instructions, Jesus sent them out two-by-two to heal the sick and cast out demons and to tell the people that the kingdom of God was at hand. In so doing, they were preparing the way of the Lord, an Elijah/John the Baptist function.

When the seventy returned, they marveled that even the demons submitted to them in Jesus' name. Jesus told them that while they were out, he saw Satan falling from heaven like lightening. Moreover, they had been given the authority to tread on serpents and scorpions. He also warned them not to get overly excited about this, but to rejoice most of all that their names were written in heaven. Jesus then prayed to God the Father and rejoiced that his followers had gotten to see the advent of the kingdom of God. Kings and prophets from many generations had longed to see what they were seeing. They were a blessed generation.

What Does the Story Mean in the Book?

How does this story function in the gospel of Luke and what are its lessons for the followers of Jesus? In terms of how the story functions within the book, it should be noted that it follows two smaller stories that focus particularly on foreshadowing Jesus' fate to come in Jerusalem (9:51–56), and on the radical commitment demanded of the follower of Jesus (9:57–62). These texts, along with our passage, function as the beginning of what is known in Lukan studies as the "travel narrative." In 9.51, Luke tells that after Jesus was done with his ministry in the northern territories in Israel, he "set his face like a flint" to go to Jerusalem to die. What follows is a long and sometimes seemingly random set of stories and teachings, unique to Luke's gospel, that are joined together (this material is unique to Luke's gospel) under the banner of Luke's travel motif. It is unclear when the travel narrative ends, but it prepares the way for Luke's vivid account of the passion week.

The purpose of this section is to prepare the disciples to take what they had learned from Jesus' ministry in and around Galilee and take the kingdom announcement and demonstration throughout Israel and then to the nations of the earth. As this material matches closely what we learn about the sending of the twelve in Luke 9, it appears that Jesus is laying down, in principle, healthy patterns for outreach activity. The meaning and application of this text, therefore, finds its home among discussions about spreading the gospel into regions that have not yet heard that the kingdom of God has drawn near in

Christ. Our passage about the sending of the seventy finds its place in evangelistic efforts to those from a different culture.

The patterns Jesus lays down have been used in missionary thrusts for two millennia and are tried and true. We see that Jesus appoints and sends those whom he selects and who are willing to go. This is not something casual and to be taken lightly. As we will see, he is the Lord of the harvest and releases his laborers in his timing. Because we are expected to ask him for laborers, he must be assuming that we are close enough to the harvesting that we know what field hands are needed and what skill-sets are required. The harvest is plentiful, meaning that many have been prepared to receive the kingdom. It is, after all, harvest season. We also note that the workers are sent out two-by-two. Practically speaking, there are many advantages to having a partner, which we will not go over here. Suffice it to say that it is vital to travel in at least twos for safety, encouragement, and because the Old Testament taught that by two or three witnesses something is confirmed. The second presenter serves to confirm the witness of the other, thereby validating his/her claims. In that culture, as the travelers go into a town, it would have been a lot like the Middle East marketplace scenes we've seen in movies. Hospitality is very important in those settings and it would have been easy to strike up conversations and to state the business at hand. This is a great passage to envision the practice of what is often called "power evangelism." Two-by-two evangelists fan out in a populated area praying for information from the Lord and stepping out on that revelation. In our text, Jesus suggests healing the sick and delivering people from demons, before announcing that in Jesus, God has acted on behalf of the world that he loves. Through his birth, life, death, resurrection, and ascension, the rule of God is now present and breaking in.

Advancing the Development of God's People

Because the full consummation of the kingdom of God is in the future and not fully realized, not all will be excited about the message of Jesus and the kingdom. Jesus said we are being sent out among wolves that would like to attack and kill Christians. Nevertheless, Jesus said, "Go!" We are to trust God's protection when we are sent on an evangelistic mission. We are also to trust God's provision, a move that requires great faith. We are not to take extra clothing, thus not giving the impression that we are on vacation. Moreover, if we see people we know along the way and engage with them, we will get off the track. No, we must remain resolute and focused, always watching for opportunities, always wary for attacks. These kinds of evangelistic and missionary endeavors will not be easy because of the warfare involved. Indeed, they will require faith at every level. This is the reason we must be sure that the Lord of the harvest is sending us. If he is, then we know that he will take care of us.

Moreover, we must establish a base of operations from which to conduct our campaigns, however long they might be. Jesus never stayed in one place too long, but that had to do with his call and the timing of his mission. We are to appreciate the hospitality we receive and eat everything given to us to honor our host, the "man of peace." In his sovereignty, God has strategically placed people in the towns and cities we will be going to. Joyful over a healing or deliverence or drawn to the messengers for reasons they don't understand, folks who love hospitality will be inclined to open their homes to the gospel messengers. Rehab, the prostitute in Jericho when Israel sent out twelve spies to scope out the land, was a classic example of a man or woman of peace. She welcomed the spies and even sheltered them from harm. When invited into a home, we are to bless the house with the peace of God. If the head of the household does not receive our blessing, God's peace will return to us. If the town itself rejects the kingdom announcement, we are to wipe the dust from our feet, or find a cultural equivalent to say that God's judgment rests on the town. We are to then move on. We are to return to those who had sent us, when the campaign is over, for a time of debriefing.

Is there a deeper sense in which to understand this text, a sense that connects it to the ongoing development of the people of God? Again, the answer is a resounding "Yes!" The would-be interpreter would have no clue about why this commissioning account would be any different from the sending of the twelve, a chapter earlier, without knowing how the narrative works. It would seem unnecessarily redundant in a book that is already pressing the limits of its scroll length to have two stories saying similar things.

The key to why both texts are needed, is the two sets of numbers. Only the reader that is beginning to connect the dots knows that Jesus chose twelve as a prophetic picture of the national resurrection of Israel as seen by Ezekiel in his vision of a valley of bones coming back to life and two sticks becoming one (Ezek 37). In the same manner, the student that knows the storyline will remember that the number seventy (or seventy-two: the Hebrew text of Genesis lists seventy nations and the Greek text lists seventy-two) is likely a reference to the number of nations sired by the three sons of Noah listed in Genesis 10, chronologically after the division of languages at Babel in Genesis 11. The big picture reader also knows that Israel's call (Gen 12.2–3; Ex 19.6; Mt 28.16–18) is to be a missionary people reaching the seventy [two] nations (the number of nations at the time Genesis was written, not the number of nations at the time of the apostles). This then means that the sending of the twelve and the seventy go together to depict the call on Israel as the people of God for the world. Those Gentiles that were originally reached by Jewish missionaries had now been grafted into the vine of the true Israel. These two texts function as an invitation to the readers to play their parts in the ongoing story of salvation for the worldwide, multinational church of Jesus Christ.

Luke understood that salvation was for the whole person. The church, therefore, is a healing community in every sense of the word. As these first generation Jewish missionaries healed the sick, they announced the arrival of the kingdom. Luke, therefore, understood Jesus' intentions in both sending accounts to function as a model for how faith communities can make inroads in communities that have not yet heard. In our modern context, we would call this "power evangelism." People are saved because they see that the end of the age has dawned and they want to be a part of the eschatological people of God. We are a community that has been and is being saved. The book of Acts will show that this culture was transmitted to the second generation. Will it be transferred to the third and so on? That is the question.

The church in which I grew up did not believe that the gifts of the Spirit, nor healing and deliverance, were for the present day. When I first read the book of Acts, I wanted to do the things the early church did. It seemed obvious to me as a new believer that the apostles were simply emulating Jesus and I wanted to do the same. When I was told that those kinds of things no longer happened today, I was both grieved and confused. Years later, in college, I had a life-changing experience of being empowered by the Holy Spirit. Immediately, my spiritual antennae were opened to the spiritual world in a new way. I began receiving information from the Lord about people that was helpful to them. I was then introduced to the more charismatic dimensions of the Christian life and realized that what I had been taught in church about the Spirit had not been entirely correct. From that time on, I pressed in to learn as much as I could about the things of the kingdom to supplement my solid evangelical heritage, for which I am deeply grateful. It gave me a rock-solid foundation for my faith.

Not long after, I was asked to teach on a staff recruiting retreat for a well-known youth organization. I taught on the kingdom of God in a way that was in alignment with the passage in Luke we are now studying. Many young people were healed of various things that weekend and the Holy Spirit empowered the group for their work of reaching high school students for Christ. A year later, one of the staff members told me that they had the most powerful year of conversions they had ever had in their region.

At lunch on that same retreat, I was told that there was a girl that wanted to see me. As I approached, she began screaming about the light and to get away from her. I immediately realized she was demonized.

At that point in my kingdom journey, I had come to believe that this world existed, but as yet had had no experience in it. The Lord picked what Americans would call a "doozy" (extreme case) for my first encounter with the demonized. I grabbed a couple of staff members and we took her to a private room and spent all afternoon praying with her. She had been a prostitute and was, in the end, delivered from seventeen demons. The staff, who were with me, had come from a background like mine, and their eyes were like saucers. By the time I had to go speak, we had gotten to a demon that called itself "the gatekeeper," whose job it was to guard what it called "the king." We were never able to get the king exorcised. It was tied to a hurt and sin that gave it legal right to be there.

Later that week, we had another session with her, and this time I recruited someone more experienced than I was. During the session, my teammate received a picture of her being raped behind some file cabinets in an office setting. The girl confessed that this was exactly what had happened to her and what had precipitated her "career move" to become a prostitute. The devil had lied to her and told her that Jesus had raped her. She believed the lie and this is what gave the demons, especially "the king," legal access to be in her. We rebuked the lie, she repented, and the king left. She was free. Let's just say that from that point on, I embraced the sending call of Jesus for his followers to announce and demonstrate the release of Isaiah 61 that Jesus had proclaimed as fulfilled in Luke 4.18-19, "The Spirit of the Lord is on me...to proclaim liberty to the captives...to set the oppressed free."

Contributions to the Cosmic Plan of God

When we macro out one more aperture setting to see what we can learn from this text about the cosmic level of redemption, again we gain further insight. Upon the return of the seventy from their mission, Jesus told them he had "seen" (a vision of) Satan "falling from heaven like lightening." The Old Testament prophets understood prophetically that before the end of the age there would be a time of final trouble, an end-time conflict between God and Satan that would result in Satan's decisive and final defeat. This understanding is ultimately based on Genesis 3.15 and the prophecy about the male child that would crush the head of the serpent. History, from that point on, was moving toward this great showdown between the powers.

These powers were defeated through the Christ event when God accomplished in the middle of history what the Jews expected at the end. In Christ, the end had broken into the present age of evil and God staked his claim on the earth.

This is why Jesus taught us to pray, "Let your kingdom come on earth as it is in heaven." Heaven was beginning to rain down in the midst of the present age of evil. No reader of the Old Testament had seen that the defeat of Satan would come in two stages, his "binding" as the strongman in the first coming of Christ and his ultimate destruction at the end of the age. Jesus saw in the ministry of the seventy a sign that one day every nation would receive the kingdom that was inaugurated by the Jews. Because the strongman had been bound in his first coming, the disciples' success in Luke and in Acts was a sign that Satan had fallen from heaven like lightening. Let us minister as those who know in Christ that Satan has been ultimately defeated.

Playing My Part in the Bigger Story of God

If I want to play my part in God's story, if I want my life to count, I must know who and where I am in "real time." It is the same way with God's people. Together we are the worldwide church of Jesus Christ and we have been given the assignment to disciple all the nations of the earth. One day, every tongue and tribe and language and nation will worship and image God. What time is it in history? Where am I? Where is my city, town, and church in regard to this assignment? This is not something new, but was the original mandate given to Abraham, fulfilled in Christ, and then given to the apostles to pass on to the second generation. We moderns belong to "Acts twenty-nine" churches, i.e., those churches established after the twenty-eight chapters in Acts. The job that began in Acts to reach the "uttermost parts of the earth" is far from finished (see the statistics in the Introduction). Furthermore, the mission will not be accomplished apart from the outpouring of a great time of trouble on the earth that will raise up a powerful, purified people. Are our churches getting its members ready to bring history to closure? Are we focused, first of all, on outreach in our local context? Is our highest mission priority penetrating the unreached peoples with the gospel? Is my community learning to suffer with dignity and integrity when we are persecuted for the gospel? Are we imaging God to the world around us by learning to love ourselves so we can love our neighbors? This last one will require an ever-growing level of self-awareness that comes only as we receive deep healing from past hurts, especially forgiving those that have harmed us. All the while, we need to take responsibility for sinning against those who have sinned against us. At the heart of it all is turning from the idols we have built, because we have repressed in our wickedness the God we know in our hearts is there as Creator-King, loving, powerful, and wise. The two passages we have just studied show how knowing the bigger story of God brings the narrative portions of Scripture to light at three different levels, at the level of the meaning of the story within its book, within the story of the people of God, and within the story of the cosmic redemption of the world.

When we know how to connect the dots and reconstruct the plotline of the Bible, what is today called the "metanarrative," we can see that there is one God, one plan, and one story. In the Bible, we see that God is establishing his kingdom through his savior for his glory. This is who he is and what he does; he doesn't do anything else. Our purpose, our objectives, our goals, our behaviors need to line up with these three great, worldview-building themes: Kingdom, Savior, and Glory. He will establish Trinitarian life and all its beauty—what the ancients called the beatific vision—through true humanity modeled by Christ and ruling perfectly over his realm.

God's plan advances as his followers speak his words and do his works (cf. Acts 1.1; Acts will be about all that Jesus will *continue* to do and teach). The "ian" in the word "Christian" is the diminutive in the language of the New Testament. It means "a little version of something." Followers of Jesus were called "Christ-ians" because they were different from the culture around them. The people around them called them "little anointed ones." When they told stories of Jesus, it became readily apparent that they were just like the stories they were telling, even when they suffered for sharing it. This does not mean they were perfect, but that they made it their highest priority to emulate their hero. They were baptized and shared in Christ's Last Supper, shared Christ and his kingdom with everyone, cared for the poor, repented, worshipped with abandon, healed the sick, and cast out demons. They took the gospel cross-culturally and planted churches. As God's people participated in the life of the local church, they discovered the things they were gifted by the Spirit to do.

As we are learning to play our parts in God's story as he is establishing his kingdom through his savior for his glory, God gives us supernatural abilities through the Holy Spirit to bless our communities of faith and to be sent out from them to the world. Just as Adam and Eve needed God's blessing to succeed in their three assignments to multiply, fill, and rule the earth as God's ambassadors, we also receive God's blessing. When we become followers of Christ, the Spirit of the Lord indwells and empowers us to live lives that reflect the image of God to the world. As we step out in ministry, God gives us repeated experiences of being empowered with the Spirit. The empowerment of the Spirit is accompanied by the release of the ability to hear from God in all kinds of ways. As we subject our will to his, we step out to take risks, partnering with him as he advances his kingdom. As we do, he releases revelatory information, showing us what he is doing so we can cooperate with him. Some of these supernatural abilities will be given to us regularly, helping us to know our role(s) among God's people. As we take risks in partnering with God, he will also give us gifts that we don't regularly operate in. These gifts are given in specific situations to enable us to succeed in multiplying, filling, and ruling. As we step out and "go for it," we learn more and more how to operate in the realm of the Spirit as we are being transformed into his image.

At the end of the age, after God separates the sheep and the goats, there will be a great banquet during which he will give rewards for lives lived in his service. True followers of Jesus live their lives to hear the words, "Well done my good and faithful servant" during this remarkable event. The Bible says that rewards will be given to those who have been faithful. To see his face, to hear "well done," and to receive rewards for serving him…makes this, in my opinion, the only life worth living. All sacrifices made and suffering incurred for him will fall into the background in that moment. We will be lost in the radiance of the face of Christ. Forever, we will hear and tell the stories of the establishment of God's kingdom, through God's savior, for his glory. Amen (may it be so).

ABOUT THE AUTHOR

Bill Jackson earned his B.A. from Wheaton College, his M.Div. from Gordon-Conwell Seminary, and his D.Miss. from Fuller Seminary. Always a New Testament specialist with a heart for world missions, Bill did his doctoral dissertation on Barriers and Breakthroughs in the book of Acts. He has started two Campus Life clubs, planted or helped to plant five Vineyard churches, and taught in seven schools. He has also written courses for Vineyard Bible Institute. Most recently he has been the academic dean and one of the principal professors for the Master of Ministry program through St. Stephen's University in New Brunswick, Canada. He is also the author of *The Quest for the Radical Middle: A History of the Vineyard*. He currently works for Radical Middle Ministries, a non-profit organization that develops resources, training, and education for empowered evangelicals. He also continues to pastor with his wife of thirty-four years, Betsy, as they oversee the "Welcome Ministry" at the Inland Vineyard in Corona, CA. Bill is a well-traveled conference speaker noted for solid biblical content and releasing ministry in the Holy Spirit. He has also traveled extensively teaching his seminar called *Nothinsgonnastopit! The Storyline of the Bible*, which traces the storyline of the Bible in seven hours. His materials and conference information are available through www.radicalmiddle.net or www. nothinsgonnastopit.com. He and his wife, Betsy, live in Corona, CA, and have three grown children, Luc, Megan, and John.

RADICAL MIDDLE MINISTRIES

For more information on resources
from Radical Middle Ministries see:

www.radicalmiddle.net
www.nothinsgonnastopit.com

CPSIA information can be obtained at www.ICGtesting.com
Printed in the USA
LVOW112116150412

277684LV00003B/1/P